COLLINS

GARDEN

Planning and Design

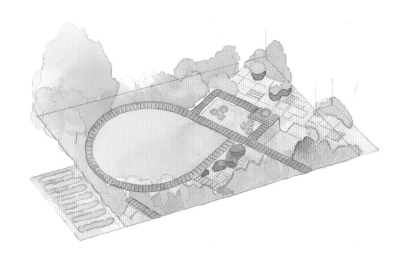

DAVID STEVENS

HarperCollins*Publishers*
London

HarperCollins*Publishers*
London

First published in 2000 by HarperCollins*Publishers*

Most of the text and illustrations in this book were previously
published in the *Collins Complete Garden Manual*

Design and layout © HarperCollins*Publishers* 1999
Text: © David Stevens 1999

A catalogue record for this book is available
from the British Library.

ISBN 0-00-414107-5

Designed and produced for HarperCollins*Publishers* by
Cooling Brown, Middlesex, England
Editorial: Carole McGlynn, Ann Kay
Design: Alistair Plumb, Tish Mills, Pauline Clarke
Photography: Peter Anderson, Steve Gorton, Matthew Ward

Colour origination: Colourscan

Printed and bound in Great Britain by Scotprint

The HarperCollins website address is:
www.**fire**and**water**.com

Contents

INTRODUCTION

❖

4

DESIGN IS VERY MUCH the buzzword of gardening at present, as the large number of television 'makeover' programmes, magazines and books bear testimony. While it is good to spread the word, remember that garden design should never be a 'quick-fix' solution, as these rarely bear the test of time, in either practical or aesthetic terms.

While many of us are confident about planning the inside of our homes, our ideas often dry up when we move outside. This is due in part to all those seemingly impossible plant names, together with the bewildering range of features and materials on display at every garden centre. Add to this the seduction of random purchases of attractive plants, container and other features, and it is little wonder that gardens can end up as a mass of unrelated features that are both unsettling on the eye and a chore to maintain. Gardens should not only reflect our needs and personality, but should link the house with the outdoor space in a pleasing overall composition.

I have worked as a landscape and garden designer for the past thirty years, over which time I have created thousands of gardens of all shapes and sizes, in both town and country settings. No two of these have ever been the same, but all

◁ **IT IS IMPORTANT** *that a garden is designed to suit your lifestyle. This raised wooden deck under a tree offers a shady retrea in a sunny climate.*

◁ A WATER FEATURE, *high on the wish list for many people's gardens, can be built into the design from an early stage.*

have been designed following a well-tried set of rules that I know will work under most circumstances. Design is not a haphazard business but a logical sequence that achieves the best out of the location and incorporates all the desired features.

There are obvious advantages to preparing a design on paper first. You can estimate the cost of materials and plants, allow contractors to tender competitively on particular areas of work, or the whole garden, or phase the construction to carry out yourself as a DIY project over as long a period as you want. In addition, there is no doubt that a well-designed garden adds value to your home.

What I hope to do in this book is to take the mystery out of design and take you though the planning sequence that I use myself. This is simple and straightforward; professionals do not waste time on unnecessary details. That is not to say that good design is bland – far from it – but the designs that work best are clear and simple. I shall also be passing on various tricks of the trade that I have learned and used over the years.

Your garden is an extremely valuable space: it should give you somewhere to relax, play, dine, entertain, grow plants and escape from the pressures of everyday life. This will probably be the largest space over which you have complete control, and its planning, while it may be challenging, should be both fun and endlessly rewarding.

DAVID STEVENS

What is good design?

A good garden design is, above all, simple yet practical. It should reflect the needs of those that use it, provide a link with the adjoining house, blend with the surrounding environment and provide colour and interest throughout the year. No two gardens are ever alike, because the requirements of each person or family are different, which in turn shapes the finished layout.

6

△ CONTRASTING
MATERIALS *produce
a strong design feature
in this paved garden.*

WHY DESIGN A GARDEN?

Design is all about control and it is this that sets any garden apart from a natural environment. Even the most seemingly random wildlife area will have been as carefully planned as a formal garden, albeit to suit a very different set of circumstances.

Working out a design allows you to create a garden that fits you like a glove, allocates a sensible budget that can be spread over a period of time and lessens the chances of over-complication from those frequent and expensive visits to the local garden centre.

◁ IN THIS
ENCLOSED *city
courtyard, a raised
timber deck supports
table and chairs,
while the central area
of the garden is laid
as stone flags. The
raised pool adds
interest and brings
soothing sounds to
mask city noises.
A small shed tucked
into the corner is
stained dark to make
it unobtrusive.*

Apart from the pleasure gained from enjoying a tailor-made space, a well-planned garden will, in all probability, add value to your home should you wish to move.

SETTING A THEME

While it is attractive to think of, say, a cottage- or an oriental-style garden, such a rigid approach can be dangerous, particularly in the initial stages of working out a design. By far the most important consideration is you and the needs of your family. There is little point in dreaming of an idyllic cottage garden then finding that you have to contend with boisterous youngsters playing football, riding bikes and generally having a good time romping through your prize delphiniums.

Remember that a garden can change its style and character over a period of time and what may start off as a tough, but hopefully good-looking, family environment, could end up a few years later as a peaceful, idyllic haven dedicated to plants.

◁ THE NEEDS OF SMALL
CHILDREN *have been catered for
by cleverly integrating a sandpit
into a paved area. It would need
to be covered when not in use.*

FORM FOLLOWS FUNCTION

A good garden is therefore one that reflects the needs of its owners in a simple and straightforward way. It should be practical but full of interest and surprises and hopefully give a real impression of space. The best designs offer mystery and surprise by dividing the area into a number of separate 'outside rooms', each one of which can have a different theme or purpose.

None of this is expensive or difficult to achieve. Most professional garden designers work to a well-tried and tested set of rules that they know will work in the majority of situations. There is nothing mysterious about these 'tricks of the trade', so observe the guidelines given in the following pages and you will achieve a garden design that really works.

▷ **BRICK STEPS** *separate the two tiers of this garden but lawned areas on both levels give continuity. The geometric design is softened by the abundant planting.*

Starting from scratch

There are advantages and disadvantages to starting with a brand new plot. The positive aspect is having a clean canvas, allowing you to plan everything exactly as you want. The down side will often be that you inherit a barren space, surrounded by stark fences and offering little in the way of screening from neighbouring windows.

8

ASKING THE RIGHT QUESTIONS

The first stage of any planning is to ask two simple questions – what do you have and what do you need? If you can answer these honestly and accurately, you will be well on the way to creating a successful garden. But first of all, if your plot is a new development, take a look at what the builders have left you. Developers usually provide a minimal amount of paving – often a few paving slabs and a path to the back door – and they may also have laid a lawn.

△ TAKE A CRITICAL LOOK AT THE BOUNDARIES, *noting the condition of fences and walls. You may decide to replace them in the final design.*

This is the time to check the quality of the soil, to ensure the builders have provided ample clean topsoil. The difference between topsoil and subsoil lies in its fertility: the former should be rich in organic matter, easily workable and able to support healthy plant growth. The subsoil, which lies beneath the topsoil, is unable to support plant growth and is usually impossible to work. But irresponsible builders may have simply dumped subsoil from the house foundations over the garden, in which case you should ask them to remove this layer of subsoil and replace it with clean topsoil.

WHAT DO YOU HAVE?

This can be assessed by carrying out a simple survey. While we shall be dealing with how to measure your garden a little later, there are a number of important factors to consider at the outset.

• Check out any existing features, including the type of fences and walls, and look at the building materials of the house itself, all of which could suggest materials for the new garden.

• See if there are any good views of which you could take advantage or – rather more common – any bad views that would need screening. Check out any changes in level that could determine the position of steps.

• Check the orientation of your plot by noting the position of the sun throughout the day. It will rise in the east and set in the west, being due south at midday, and the path it takes across your garden will suggest the best place to site a patio, pool, summer house or greenhouse, as well as where to grow vegetables and position planting that enjoys bright or shady conditions. If in doubt, use a compass.

• Find out just what kind of soil you have, whether it is acid or alkaline, as this will

△ USE A SOIL TESTING METER *to check what type of soil you have. Be sure to take samples in several places, as the soil can vary in different areas around the garden.*

△ **LAYING OUT THE BONES OF A GARDEN** *and constructing it in stages helps you to realize its full potential.*

determine the type of plants that will flourish in your garden. This assessment is best carried out over some months; if you are prepared to take a full year, you will see changes wrought by the seasons and the pattern of shadows cast by buildings or trees, and will start to get a feel for your own space that will be invaluable when you come to prepare the design.

WHAT DO YOU WANT?

Assemble a list of your needs and desires over a period of time, throwing the discussion open to the whole family: after all, everyone will use the space in one way or another. Your wish list will, of course, depend on the available space but a typical list might include lawn, patio, pool, barbecue, swing, slide, shed, greenhouse, salad crops, fruit, shrub and herbaceous planting and rockery. If the list seems too long, you can reduce it later: the important thing is not to leave anything out at the planning stage.

THE ORDER OF WORK

Only once you have completed the design can you plan the construction of the garden, but it is as well to consider a logical order of work at this stage. The creation of the garden will be divided between the 'hard landscape', comprising paving, walls, fences, paths and any other permanent features, and the 'soft landscape', including lawn and planting.

The hard landscape is generally tackled first. It makes sense to work out from the house ends, initially laying the patio or terrace, which may incorporate raised beds, overhead beams, built-in barbecue and seating. Electric cables, run through conduit, should be set below the paved area before work starts; enlist the help of a professional electrician first. Think also about the provision of an outside tap for taking water down the garden.

In a sloping garden a terrace can link into steps, which in turn will give way to any paths that lead down the garden. If a

new fence or wall is needed, make this a priority, to provide shelter and screening.

If no lawn was laid by the developer, this will be the next job, with any island beds accurately cut out and cultivated. You can then erect an arch or pergola and install any garden buildings. Besides a patio, think about providing a simple concrete or paved work area round a shed or greenhouse: it will be invaluable for parking a wheelbarrow, organizing tools and allowing you to carry out a multitude of outdoor jobs. Paving is also practical in front of a summer house or beneath an arbour. Finally, you can think about the inclusion of other major features, such as a rockery or a pool.

In terms of the soft landscape, place trees first, securely staked and tied, followed by shrubs, herbaceous plants and ground cover. Mulch beds with bark to preserve moisture while plants establish. Use boards to protect a new lawn from both feet and barrows.

Developing an existing garden

Moving into an established garden means that, instead of starting with a clean canvas, you will inherit features built to suit circumstances entirely different from your own. It is important not to feel constrained by this but, on the other hand, think carefully before getting rid of established trees and shrubs that have taken a long time to grow. Maturity is not something you can instantly replace.

10

ASSESSING WHAT IS THERE

When a garden has been designed for another family it may initially seem fine, but does it really suit you? If it has been well looked after, the temptation is to leave things the way they are, or simply to tack new features on to the existing layout in an attempt to make it more appropriate for you. But compromise rarely works: your first job should be to take a good, hard look at what is there and decide exactly what you would like to keep and what you want to remove.

Classic examples of existing elements you need to re-consider might include a vegetable plot that you do not have the time to maintain, borders that are either too big for you to manage or too small for the plants you want to grow, a pool that could be a hazard for young children or simply the lack of a big enough patio for your family to eat outdoors.

It makes sense to carry out the basic survey in exactly the same way as for a brand new garden, but there will be many more features to measure and take note of. It is important to check the position of existing trees and other large plants, identifying them if you can. You may want to keep some and move others, supplementing them with plants of your own choice. List all the additional features you wish to include.

ADDING AND SUBTRACTING

The most radical measures may involve removing a tree that has outgrown its position or that casts too much shade; rebuilding or extending of a patio or breaking up paving to establish a lawn in its place; laying new paths to provide better access around the garden and to double as a hard surface for wheeled toys. If you have young children, you may need to install securely fixed play equipment where it can be clearly seen from the house.

If you wish to introduce a summer house, a greenhouse or a shed, their position will depend on the layout of the garden and, in the case of a greenhouse, the course of the sun throughout the day. You may want to

△ **ADVANTAGE IS TAKEN** *of a sloping site to create a series of pools, linked by a soothing waterfall. Lush planting along the banks, including irises, ligularias and euphorbias, softens the pool edges and reinforces the garden's watery feel.*

▽ **IN THIS INFORMAL,** *low-maintenance design, sun-loving plants flop out over the gravel surface, while the sundial acts as a focal point.*

◁ **A GENTLE TRANSITION** *is provided in this garden, from the hard-surfaced patio to the softly planted borders at the far end. The mature apple trees have great character and have been left as a feature of the lawn.*

Often the first view of an existing garden is one of an overgrown wilderness; however tempting it may be, never adopt a 'slash and burn' policy, as there will almost certainly be some trees and shrubs that are well worth keeping. While it makes sense to root out brambles and other invaders as soon as possible, take your time over everything else and get to know the garden before embarking on drastic reshaping. If possible, leave it for several seasons to see what plants come up.

RENOVATING

As with a new garden, it is sensible to renovate any hard landscaping first and to embark on a programme of getting everything back into condition. Paving can be re-laid or simply re-pointed, fences and walls should be checked over for sturdiness and weather-proofing and pools must cleaned out if they are badly silted up. Beds can then be tidied and the soil improved by the addition of well-rotted organic matter. At the appropriate time of year, shrubs can be pruned, hardy perennials divided, climbers thinned and neatly tied into trellis or horizontal wires and lawns started on their own renovation programme.

Leave some framework plants in a border to give the impression of maturity while your new plants develop. You can take them out later if you do not want them. Or, to provide a young border with an established look, plant fast-growing species like buddleja, broom and mallow; remove these in due course if you wish.

ON THE MOVE

❖

Rather than getting rid of plants that are in the wrong place, move them to a better one. Take out a large, deciduous shrub in the winter by carefully digging around its base and sliding it on to a polythene sack with as much root as possible. Slide the sack across the lawn or paving and place the shrub into a well-prepared hole so that the new soil level matches the old. Water well, staking it if it is in a windy position, and cut the stems back by about half.

incorporate, or to remove, a vegetable or herb garden, site a rock garden on a sunny slope, or perhaps include a pool. You might decide to set a pergola over an existing path or tuck a gazebo into a distant corner. And you can reduce, increase or simply re-organize existing planting. All new features must be positioned in relation to the existing layout, unless you conclude that the layout simply will not work for you, in which case the design must be modified in order to incorporate your new ideas.

If a small lawn is in poor condition, consider paving it over to reduce maintenance and increase sitting space. On the other hand, if there is too much paving, you may want to replace it with lawn and planting, in which case you must remove all the old surface and the foundations beneath raised beds or other features. You will have to break up and thoroughly cultivate the underlying soil to improve drainage, forking in well-rotted manure or compost. For shrubs and general planting you need to import 45cm (18in) of clean topsoil; for a lawn this depth can be reduced to a minimum of 15cm (6in).

Design considerations

The checklist which you and your family drew up will now be invaluable in working out just what you can fit in and putting the various features in order of importance. A patio might well be top of the list, with a lawn, particular types of planting, a barbecue and a pool following on. Some items at the end of the list may have to be left out but prioritizing your needs in this way will help to focus your design more clearly.

12

△ **A KITCHEN GARDEN** *need not be tucked out of sight: it may be more practical near the house.*

SIZE

The size of the garden will obviously have a bearing on just how many or how few features you can include. A large space could be sub-divided into separate garden 'rooms' or areas, separated by walls, hedges or trellis, each space having a different style, purpose or type of planting. A garden compartmentalized in this way will display the classic elements of mystery and surprise, leading you to wonder just what is around the corner or in the next room, and this naturally provides a sense of greater space.

Small plots effectively concentrate the mind on just what you want to include, as there will definitely not be room for

everything. While most people consider a patio or sitting area essential, it does diminish the area available for planting, unless you incorporate raised beds. Think carefully about how important a lawn is in a small space; you may decide that the area will have more unity if it is entirely paved, with plant-filled containers, raised beds and climber-clad boundary walls providing the essential softening elements.

BUDGET

One of the great advantages of working to a plan is that you can allocate a sensible budget over a period of time, by building the garden in stages over

several seasons or even years. The hard landscape elements of paving, fencing, walling and paths will take the lion's share of the budget, representing up to 75 per cent of the total cost. This means that it is essential to get the design right in the first place, since mistakes could be expensive to rectify. Plants and planting are a relatively inexpensive part of the finished garden and, if you are a keen gardener, can be propagated or grown from seed at minimal cost.

THE FUNCTION OF A GARDEN

The prime function of a garden is to meet the needs of you and your family and the secret is to allocate space logically so that one activity does not disrupt another. This means having ample room for sitting and dining, preferably close to the house, possibly divided by a low wall or planting from the lawn, where ball games and all kinds of play can take place. Space permitting, this might in turn give way to fruit, vegetables and space for a working or utility area. One of the most important aspects of garden design is to ensure that all areas are linked by paths that give access in all weathers, leading the eye in a pleasing way from one part of the garden to another.

◁ **IN THIS FORMAL DESIGN**, *trellis and low hedging are the elements used to divide up the garden. The box hedges provide a crisp edge, framing the planting as well as separating the 'rooms'.*

AGE AND ABILITY

No garden need remain unchanged throughout its life. The key is to build a garden that can be added to and modified as your lifestyle alters, without changing the underlying structure. This might mean that a toddler's sandpit becomes a raised bed or pool, while tough 'ball-proof' planting could be replaced by more delicate species once young children have grown up. A lawn could give way to an area of loose cobbles, gravel and planting, requiring little maintenance for busy people.

13

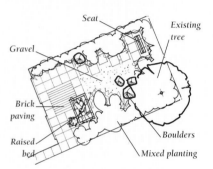

Seat
Gravel
Existing tree
Brick paving
Boulders
Raised bed
Mixed planting

WORKING PERSON WITH NO CHILDREN

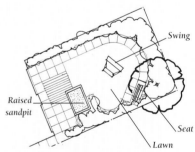

Swing
Raised sandpit
Seat
Lawn

COUPLE WITH GROWING CHILDREN

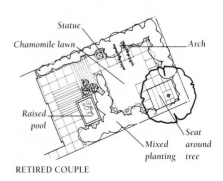

Statue
Chamomile lawn
Arch
Raised pool
Seat around tree
Mixed planting

RETIRED COUPLE

PRACTICALITIES

Remember that a garden has to include the utilitarian as well as the beautiful. It makes sense to group certain practical items together, such as a shed, greenhouse, compost and incinerator, and contain them within a hard-surfaced working area of ample size. They could then be neatly screened from the rest of the garden with trellis or hidden behind a 'wing' of planting.

Washing lines are usually essential and will need easy access by a path; some can be housed in a reel attached to the house wall so that they can be neatly stored when not in use. Dustbins can be kept in a purpose-built store with hinged doors and top. Remember to fit a sandpit with a removable cover that could double as a play surface as well as discouraging nocturnal visitors.

△ CLEVERLY POSITIONED *wall mirrors, perhaps framed by a false arch or trellis, can dramatically increase the feeling of space.*

SMALL-SCALE SOLUTIONS

❖

- Garden buildings such as sheds take up a lot of space but you may be able to incorporate storage alongside or beneath a built-in barbecue, or design overhead beams, smothered with climbers, to frame a potting bench that doubles as a tool store.

- Raised beds maximize the planting area while their retaining walls can double as built-in seating.

- If the sound and movement of water is a priority, bear in mind that a wall-mounted or millstone water feature takes up far less space than a pool.

Garden styles

Style should never be confused with fashion, which is a passing fad, usually with little substance. It can be dangerous to simply 'lift' a style which was born in another country or set of circumstances and superimpose it on your garden because it can all too easily end up a pastiche. But if you are influenced by a particular garden style, it is possible to make a sensitive but practical interpretation of it. The essential point about style is that it should be your own.

14

△ **A CRISP WOODEN DECK** *is the perfect link between indoors and out in this modern garden.*

FORMAL STYLES

Strictly formal gardens rely on symmetry of design, where one side mirrors the other, using planting, lawns, clipped hedges, pools, screens and other elements in a geometric layout. Such designs often look their best adjoining a period home with a formal facade. They can be equally appropriate in small town gardens whose design becomes like that of a stage set, to be viewed from the front. Formal gardens have a naturally 'static' feel and you are guided through them by the position of the various features. While they can be extremely elegant, and are ideal for dividing into 'rooms', they are unlikely to suit a young family needing plenty of open space for play and other activities.

INFORMAL STYLES

Informal gardens come in all guises and while the best are well laid out to suit a wide range of needs, the worst are a haphazard jumble of features. In a good design there is a logical progression through the space, from a terrace or patio that has a unity with the house to the more distant areas of the garden. There should be a feeling of movement that detracts from the garden's rectangular boundaries. Features and focal points should be carefully placed to draw you through the garden and the planting should have a soft, naturalistic feel to it. Above all, this is a family-friendly style of garden.

THE PLANT LOVER'S GARDEN

A plant enthusiast's garden can take any form but most of its space will be devoted to planting beds. It is a mistake to think that such gardens favour planting at the expense of everything else, as many elegantly architectural designs, with a strong structure provided by hard landscaping, provide the perfect foil for plant form and for the texture and colour of foliage and flowers. Nor do such gardens need to contain a huge range of species, since many plant lovers are specialist growers, revelling in the characteristics of a single or limited number of plant families, such as alpines or roses. Into this same category come colour-themed gardens, foliage gardens or those devoted to sun- or shade-loving plants. Such gardens can be large or small, rural or urban, but by their very nature they tend to be places for tending and viewing rather than for boisterous play.

COTTAGE GARDENS

This romantic style of English garden, evocative of past traditions, needs more maintenance than many people imagine. And, because it relies heavily on herbaceous plants that die down in the winter, it can look very thin for half the year. But if you want a cottage garden, try framing the beds with low, evergreen hedges, such as box, to provide winter structure and include some evergreens, such as euphorbias and hellebores, among the perennials to add form and extend the display.

△ **THE SYMMETRY** *of this formal garden is used to divide it into 'rooms'. Trellis panels and clipped box frame the entrance to the lawn area while the focal statue is flanked by box spheres.*

◁ IN THIS COTTAGE-STYLE *garden, a rich combination of plants spill out profusely from the borders in a wonderfully informal display. The paths impose some structure on the design.*

GARDENS FOR WILDLIFE

❖

Over recent years there has been a trend towards growing native species of trees, shrubs and wildflowers in order to encourage wildlife into the garden. This environmentally-oriented garden is always informal in style, tending towards the wild, as it involves letting grass grow longer and leaving plants to develop seedheads and hips rather than cutting them down when they finish flowering. Provided you match species carefully to the soil type and local conditions, the planting will need little irrigation and mean lower maintenance.

ORIENTAL STYLE

A Japanese style of garden is probably the hardest to copy, partly because it looks deceptively simple. Unless you are fully versed in the deeply religious philosophy involved, which invests each plant or rock with meaning and its placing with great significance, there is a danger that your oriental-style garden will end up a pastiche of the real thing.

By all means, gain inspiration by looking at the simple yet exquisite

◁ THIS SUNNY, MEDITERRANEAN *garden is based on a Moorish theme. Container-grown citrus trees frame the rill that drops into the pool, while ceramic tiles decorate a whitewashed wall.*

detailing of the surfaces and structures of Japanese gardens, such as a raked gravel floor or the beautifully tied knots on fence panels. You will learn the vital lesson that simplicity is everything in terms of design. You could use elements like well-placed, smooth boulders or a 'river' of loose stones to simulate a dry stream bed and find pleasure in creating a simple but perfect composition.

MEDITERRANEAN STYLE

There is an intimacy to Mediterranean gardens that has to do with sunny courtyards, shade-giving overhead beams clad with climbers and warm terracotta tiles. And with the effects of global warming, such gardens are starting to look and feel right in many other parts of the world too. The most appropriate planting is fragrant and

drought-tolerant, including aromatic herbs like rosemary, lavender and thyme. Suitable plant species include many with grey, felted leaves, such as senecio and phlomis, or with the sword-like form of yuccas and phormiums, all of which have a low rate of transpiration that makes them ideal in hot, dry conditions.

MODERNIST AND MINIMAL STYLES

Since garden design is about simplicity, if you have a fondness for modernist styles, why not think in minimalist terms? A swathe of gravel, with a few architectural plants piercing through, adjoining an area of crisp paving or decking, could look superb. With large-foliage plants, such as *Vitis coignetiae* or *Fatsia japonica*, or the delicate tracery of Japanese maples against a white-painted wall, nothing more would be needed.

Drawing up a plan

Despite what you may have heard, it is quite impossible to design a garden on the back of an envelope. The plan is the foundation for all that follows, allowing you to work out the construction in stages, to give an accurate estimate of the materials needed or to brief one or more contractors to quote in competition. At a later stage it will provide you with the basis of your planting plan.

16

MEASURING UP

Surveying the garden is a simple job and one that is quite fun to do. You need some basic equipment, including a 30m (100ft) tape measure (this can be hired if necessary), a pad of paper, a pencil and a clipboard, a skewer or metal pin and a magnetic compass to check the orientation. First sketch a rough outline of the house and garden on a sheet of paper. Then start measuring as shown below, transferring the dimensions clearly to your sketch.

TAKING MEASUREMENTS

Fix the tape to a fence or boundary close to the building, unreeling it across the width of the garden to the opposite fence.

Lay the tape on the ground and take 'running' measurements across the building: include all windows, doors, drains and manholes.

Reel in the tape, then repeat the operation, this time running down the length of the garden, away from and at right angles to the house, noting the position of any features, trees or planting.

△ CHECK THE
HEIGHT *of existing steps or retaining walls. You can also get a rough idea of the fall on sloping land using a tape measure – and your eye.*

△ UNLESS YOU
HAVE A HELPER
use a skewer to fix the end of a tape in the ground. Then take running measurements, starting with one corner of the house.

CHANGES OF LEVEL

A slope away or up from the house will need measuring as this may determine the position of steps, a ramp or other features such as a split-level pool. If you have an architect's drawing of the house and garden, this will clearly show levels; otherwise existing steps or retaining walls can easily be measured and added together. On downward-sloping land, you could run out a tape at right angles, and horizontally, from a fixed point and measure the distance down to ground level to get a rough idea of the fall. In a large garden you may need the help of a professional surveyor.

PREPARING A SCALE DRAWING

When you have finished measuring up, transfer the information to a scale drawing that will become the basis for your design. This is made easier if you use squared graph paper, taking one or more squares to represent each metre or foot. Draw in the exact shape of the house and the line of garden boundaries and plot the position of existing plants and other features you intend to retain.

DRAWING UP THE DESIGN

The benefit of taking your time over preparing the survey is that it allows you to assess just what you have and to form an idea of what you want. You will start to get a real feeling for your garden and may also begin to formulate an approximate layout in your head.

Once you are ready to commit yourself to paper, do not crystallize your ideas too soon: at this stage just sketch in roughly what features will go where. If, for example, the rear of the house gets the sun for most of the day, this will be the obvious place to site a patio, with possibly a built-in barbecue and maybe some raised beds or a pool. A path could then sweep away down the garden, running across or curving around a lawn, pausing at a seat before leading to the more distant parts of the garden, which might well include the utility or working area. Make sure that paths connect and give access to all parts of the garden. Other features on your priority list, such as a play area, a summer house, an arch or a pergola, can be roughly positioned at this stage, together with any steps or walls.

It is usually a good idea to do several alternative layouts to show the family. Once everyone is happy with a layout, firm it up by making a final working drawing. Do not overwork the design or try to fit too many things in: simplicity is the key to a successful design.

TRIANGULATION

If a feature, such as a tree, is in a freestanding position that is not easily measured by running a tape down or across the garden, you can employ a technique called triangulation to plot its position; this can also be used to plot the line of boundaries that are out of square. Triangulation involves running out a tape from two previously measured points (which could be either end of the house) to the feature and noting the distances on your survey drawing. Transfer these distances to a scale drawing using a pair of compasses extended to the scaled-down measurements: the position of the tree is where the two arcs intersect. Note also the position of any trees overhanging from a neighbour's garden: their shade could influence where you site a feature.

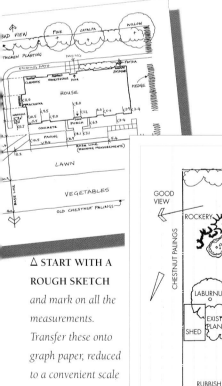

△ **START WITH A ROUGH SKETCH** *and mark on all the measurements. Transfer these onto graph paper, reduced to a convenient scale of 1:100 or 1:50; mark on all the existing features you will keep.*

Dealing with problem sites

Not all gardens are a simple rectangle: like people, they come in all shapes and sizes. This often gives them an individual character and what can at first seem like an awkward or uncompromising shape may have the potential, with the right treatment, to be turned into a garden of real distinction.

The key to an interesting garden is our ability to move through the space so that not everything is visible at a single glance. While it is possible to divide up a garden that is longer than it is broad into individual areas, other shapes of plot can present real problems.

SQUARE PLOTS
Square plots tend to be completely static, with the surrounding boundaries seeming particularly dominant. The first job will be to soften and screen the boundaries and one way this can be done is with climbing plants. A good design solution is to base the whole garden on a bold, circular pattern that sets up a real feeling of space and movement. Another 'trick of the trade' is to design the garden on diagonal lines, which provides the greatest distance across the plot. It can therefore be very effective to turn the whole design at 45° to the house and the boundaries.

WIDE PLOTS
Gardens that are wider than they are long can feel very restrictive, even when they are of a reasonable size, because of the closeness of the opposite boundary. Never place a focal point on this boundary as the eye will immediately be drawn to it, which foreshortens the space. Sit in your

△ **A CIRCULAR DESIGN** *makes the most of a square space, opening it up and leading the eye out to its perimeter.*

favourite chair in the living room, look out into the garden and assess how far down the garden you can see to either side. This is the place for a focal point as it will draw the eye away from the nearest boundary and down the garden.

DOG-LEG
Gardens that disappear around a corner are fun, but the reality is that most people ignore the valuable extra space, concentrating simply on the part they can see. The trick is to encourage movement into the area, by sweeping a path or pergola from one section to the other. This provides that vital ingredient of mystery, of wondering what lies beyond, and once you are in the new 'room' a whole new garden opens up.

DEALING WITH A SLOPE
While a gentle bank has all kinds of possibilities, a steep slope can be both daunting and expensive to deal with. If you wish to have level planting areas, you could create a series of terraces but building the necessary retaining walls is a skilled job, best left to a specialist

contractor. The design possibilities are increased, however, as such walls can be built to include steps, water features and split-level beds.

SCREENING BAD VIEWS
In town gardens it is all too common to have a bad view or to be overlooked by neighbours' windows. A carefully positioned tree, garden building or planting on the boundary will often provide the perfect screen or privacy. Remember too the screening potential of a pergola, archway or overhead beams.

△ **TRELLIS PANELS** *can be used to boost the height of a fence or wall in order to obliterate unwelcome views or mask urban surroundings.*

▷ **CLEVER USE** *has been made of the change in level in a tiny garden by creating a series of gravel-paved terraces ornamented by pots. Brick steps lead down from the ground floor of the house.*

19

Fencing and trellis

While timber fences form the boundaries of most gardens, trellis is used more as a divider, to separate different 'rooms' or to screen a utility area. There are many styles of fence, from robust panels to more open kinds that can be tailored to a specific design or situation. Trellis is either square- or diamond-patterned, in various sizes. Rot is the enemy of timber in the garden, so treat fences regularly with a non-toxic preservative.

20

CHOOSING A STYLE

Boundaries should provide shelter, security, privacy and screening, without being too imposing; more often than not they are quickly obscured by planting. Think about the overall design of the garden and its surroundings and choose a style of fence or trellis accordingly. A crisp, ranch-style fence will look fine adjoining a modern house, while close-board is more suitable in a traditional setting and wattle hurdles or a picket fence would be ideal around a cottage garden. Although the range of fence styles is wide, you could still design your own, using vertical boards in varying widths and heights to build up an elegant and durable pattern. If necessary, use re-cycled timber and paint the fence, to keep the cost down.

If you are lucky enough to have a good view you will want to retain this by keeping the fence low, or using an open style such as post and rail, but in most town gardens you will be looking for a solid boundary at a reasonable cost (see box, opposite).

More expensive, close-boarded fences are built on site, using vertically set, overlapping, 'feather-edged' boards nailed to horizontal arris rails that are morticed into posts set about 1.8m (6ft) apart. The bottom of the fence often stops 15cm (6in) above ground level with a replaceable gravel-board set beneath. Close-boarded fences will last for about 20 years.

Other options include traditional picket fences, which are most appropriate for cottage front gardens, and vertically- or diagonally-slatted ranch-style fences that have a modern, more architectural feel. All use slats fixed to horizontal rails, morticed into posts. The gaps left between the slats and the varied width of the slats themselves set up an interesting rhythm.

▷ **NEAT TRELLIS PANELS** *can become a focal point in their own right.*

◁ **CRISP PICKET FENCES** *always associate well with planting.*

Wattle or osier hurdles, originally used for penning livestock, can create an excellent low-key boundary and an ideal background for developing plants. They come in panels of varying widths and heights up to 1.8m by 1.8m (6ft by 6ft), wired to round posts; their maximum life is about ten years.

TRELLIS

The basic trellis design uses an open framework of wooden strips to form see-through boundaries or internal

◁ **HAND-WOVEN WATTLE HURDLES** *have a wonderful texture and create a suitably natural-looking background for plants in a rural garden, seen here covered with* Hedera helix *'Goldheart'.*

METAL SPIKES

❖

You can buy square metal sleeves, fitted with a spike, to hold fence posts. Drive the spike into the ground, ensuring sleeves are upright, and slot the posts into them, setting out the run as described opposite.

garden screens. It is often used in conjunction with another boundary, such as on top of a fence or wall to increase its height. Trellis panels come in a wide range of sizes and the tops may be flat or curved, or sometimes a more interesting shape. The more expensive styles of trellis use a more complex combination of slats of different thicknesses and spacing, in square or diagonal patterns. Trellis is available in natural form or painted or stained in different colours, in a wide range of non-toxic finishes.

The top of trellis can be finished with finials and cappings but always beware of over-complicating the end result. Fix freestanding trellis panels or those on the top of walls and fences to vertical posts. Trellis can also be fixed against a wall, using spacers such as cotton reels to keep it clear of the surface in order to minimize rot; use brass or stainless steel screws to prevent rust. All forms of trellis make a good host for climbing plants, offering them support.

△ **TRELLIS MAKES** *a great garden divider: it provides low-cost screening, support for climbers and allows light through to plants on either side.*

BUDGET BOUNDARIES

A fence is one of the more expensive items in a garden so it makes sense to choose carefully. The cheapest option is strands of wire stretched between metal or concrete posts, but this offers nothing in the way of privacy or shelter and will be of little use in containing youngsters or pets.

The most economic solid fence uses panels, usually 1.8m (6ft) long and in various heights up to 1.8m (6ft), set between timber or concrete posts. Made up of interwoven or overlapping laths of thin timber (*see right*), they come complete with a protective top rail. The panels are ready-treated against rot but often need toning down with a darker, non-toxic stain to prevent them looking too garish. If well maintained they should last up to 20 years.

ERECTING A FENCE PANEL

Panels can be either fixed between timber posts 7.5cm (3in) square or slotted between ready-made concrete posts, the latter being more durable. The process of erection is similar for both.

Work out the spacing of posts before you start, then clear the ground along the fence line and dig the first post hole 30cm (1ft) square and 60cm (2ft) deep. Fill the bottom of the hole with compacted hardcore so that for a 1.8m (6ft) fence the post stands 1.9m (6ft 2in) out of the ground. This will allow the bottom of the fence to sit slightly proud of ground level to prevent rot. Put in the post and fill around it with a semi-dry concrete mix, bringing the mix slightly above ground level to shed water away from the post. Check that the post is vertical and fix it with a temporary strut.

Once the first post is in position, mark out the rest of the run with a builder's line and repeat the operation.

△ **CONCRETE FENCE POSTS** *have a long life and are slotted to accept ready-made wooden fence panels.*

Boundary and retaining walls

Walls are the most permanent and expensive of all garden boundaries. Built properly from materials that are in keeping with their immediate surroundings, they can look very handsome. Walls provide excellent security, need little maintenance and will last a lifetime. Keep their design as simple as possible.

△ **DRY STONE WALLS** *have a naturally strong local character but building them is a skilled job.*

STYLES AND HEIGHT

The best walls are built from local materials, usually brick or stone. But you should not ignore the potential of crisp concrete blocks that may be cement-rendered, colour-washed or neatly pointed to produce a more contemporary style of wall that would be just right for a modern home built from similar materials. As walls are a long-term investment, choose your materials carefully, ensuring they are appropriate to the surroundings, of the best quality and built to the highest possible standards. The folly of using brick or concrete outside an old stone cottage should be obvious. There are many imitation stone walling products and they are much cheaper than the real thing, but while some of these look reasonable, many do not.

Decide on the wall's height, to offer either complete privacy or to allow a view. Certain materials, such as stone, laid dry, should only be used on walls up to a maximum of 1m (3ft) high. Brick is the most versatile material for most situations, coming in many colours from a soft yellow to terracotta. As long as you are reasonably competent, you can build a brick wall yourself; if in any doubt, or when dealing with retaining walls over 1m (3ft) high, enlist the professional help of a landscape designer or structural engineer.

△ **CONCRETE IS** *the stone of the twentieth century and can be used in numerous innovative ways. Its beauty lies in its strength and its ability to be cast to virtually any shape.*

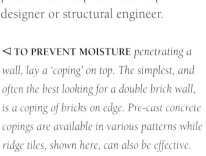

◁ **TO PREVENT MOISTURE** *penetrating a wall, lay a 'coping' on top. The simplest, and often the best looking for a double brick wall, is a coping of bricks on edge. Pre-cast concrete copings are available in various patterns while ridge tiles, shown here, can also be effective.*

△ BRICK HAS A CRISP, ARCHITECTURAL FEEL *which can help to furnish a visual link with an adjoining building. In this situation it has been used to build retaining walls for the raised beds as well as for the step and mowing edge, providing overall continuity in the garden.*

BRICK BONDS

In order to make a double brick wall as strong as possible, lay the bricks in a 'bond', so they interlock with one another. Flemish bond is the most common bond for brick walls but English and garden wall bonds are slightly stronger and look more attractive. If building a double brick wall in stretcher bond, use galvanized butterfly ties to ensure its strength.

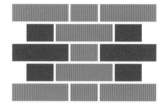

Flemish bond

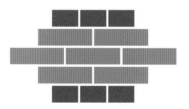

Garden wall bond

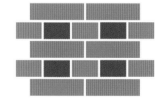

English bond

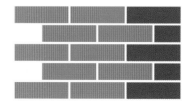

Stretcher bond

HOW A BRICK WALL IS BUILT

Walls can be built either one or two bricks thick. While the former will be quicker to build and use less bricks, it will not be as strong as a 'bonded' brick wall of double thickness. Never build a single-thickness wall more than 1m (3ft) high unless you incorporate single or double brick piers every 1.8m (6ft). Any wall, of whatever type, should be built on top of a suitable foundation or 'footing', which must be absolutely level. Its depth will vary, depending on the type of soil and the height of the wall, but it should be at least 25cm (10in) deep and twice as wide as the finished wall.

MORTAR PRECAUTION

Use a suitable mortar mix of four parts soft sand to one part cement with the addition of a 'plasticizer'. Remember that the cement used in mortar is alkaline (chalky) and if any is left at the base of a wall, it will raise the pH of the soil, making it different from elsewhere in the garden and, quite possibly, unsuitable for plant growth. This also applies to lime mortar that may be raked out of an old wall before repointing. Lay boards at ground level to catch any dropped mortar, which can then be removed.

Hedges as boundaries and features

Hedges usually form the most cost-effective boundary. They take time to establish but, once mature, they look superb. The style of hedge should take its cue from the surrounding garden: whereas precision-clipped yew will look right in a formal layout, the much looser habit of Rosa rugosa would be ideal for a softly planted country garden.

24

△ HEDGES HAVE *a naturally softer outline than walls and can be formally clipped or allowed to grow in a looser manner. Depending on the plant used, they may be squared, scalloped or easily trained into arches, like the beech hedge shown here.*

FORMAL OR INFORMAL?

Formal hedges are clipped to produce a crisp and regular outline, producing an architectural feature in a geometric layout. They can be either high, using species such as yew, beech or hornbeam to enclose the site, or low, including box, lavender and *Lonicera nitida*, acting as a framework for a geometric pattern at ground level.

Informal hedges are allowed to grow naturally, remaining unclipped, or at most loosely trained, to reveal their informal character. Many species make ideal candidates for such a treatment, though they take up rather more room than a clipped hedge. *Rosa rugosa, R. eglanteria* and many shrub roses are suitable, along with a wide selection of flowering shrubs that include choisya, potentilla, escallonia and berberis. In a rural garden you can plant a mixed hedge, using species native to the area, which might include hawthorn, blackthorn, wild dogwood and viburnum as well as hazel and elder. Such a field hedge would provide an excellent habitat for wildlife.

EVERGREEN OR DECIDUOUS?

Evergreen hedges, such as yew, holly, escallonia and laurel not only make excellent boundaries but also act as efficient windbreaks. Beech, although deciduous, holds on to its dead leaves throughout the winter, also providing a year-round screen. Although deciduous hedges are at their best in the summer, the framework of branches still provides protection and security during the winter.

∇ IN A 'COUNTRY' HEDGE *like this hawthorn boundary, you can allow the odd sapling to grow out into a tree.*

HEDGE CLIPPING

❖

When clipping a formal hedge, make it slightly wedge-shaped, with the top just narrower than the bottom. This will ensure that ample light reaches the base and that the foliage is thick right down to ground level.

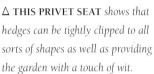

△ **THIS PRIVET SEAT** *shows that hedges can be tightly clipped to all sorts of shapes as well as providing the garden with a touch of wit.*

SPEED OF GROWTH

Given the right planting conditions and good aftercare, most hedges will establish quickly but some are quicker than others. The fastest of all are the conifers, *Chamaecyparis lawsoniana* and x *Cupressocyparis leylandii*, which can easily put on 30–45cm (12–18in) a year. They are greedy feeders, take enormous amounts of nutrients from the ground and, if left unclipped, grow to a huge height very quickly. The secret is to keep them rigorously clipped once they have reached the height you want. Plant these hedges only if you need to establish a boundary quickly and are prepared for the consequences and maintenance involved. Privet is another thug of the hedging world and exactly the same rules apply – use with caution!

Medium-fast growers include beech and hornbeam, while escallonia and

DWARF HEDGES

Low-growing hedges are ideal for framing beds at ground level. They can be clipped to heights of 15–45cm (6–18in) and may be either evergreen or flowering. Lavender is a good example of a flowering hedge and the low-growing *Berberis thunbergii* 'Atropurpurea Nana' also makes an attractive edger. Box (*see below*) forms the classic, formally clipped low hedge, while *Lonicera nitida* can create a neat border at heights up to 1m (3ft).

BUDGET HEDGES

The cost of any plant is usually related to its size at the time of planting, its speed of growth and the ease or difficulty of propagating it. Relatively slow growers, such as box or yew, are therefore at the top end of the price range. If you go direct to a nursery you can often buy 'bare-root' hedging plants which can be planted only during the dormant season. These are usually small, but correspondingly cheap. Container-grown varieties can be planted at any time of year but are generally more expensive.

griselinia are an excellent choice for gardens close to the sea. Most informal hedges, using shrubs like osmanthus or viburnum, are relatively fast developers. Yew is not as slow-growing as people think, although it is not always the best choice for a hedge because it has toxic berries and foliage. The secret of success is thorough ground preparation before planting: dig a trench, 30cm (12in) deep, then fill it with a mix of good topsoil and organic material such as well-rotted manure or compost. This planting technique applies to all hedges.

Making the most of grass

Grass forms the most important surface of English-style and country gardens. Pleasing to the eye, it is also tough, easy to shape and relatively straightforward to maintain. It provides a soft background for the widest possible range of activities. Quality is a matter of choice, from a near-perfect bowling green to a utility-grade that takes children's play and ball games in its stride.

26

SHAPE AND SIZE

In gardens where the lawn occupies the largest area, it will also be the most dominant element visually. It will play an important part in the overall design and, depending on its shape, has the ability to lead the eye away from geometric boundaries, sweep through an area in a series of strong, flowing curves or act as a classic rectangular space in a formal layout. Keep lawn shapes simple and, if using curves, never resort to the practice of hurling a hosepipe on the ground, kicking it around 'until you have a pleasing shape', then cutting out the resulting mess. Draw curves with a compass when preparing a design, one flowing into another and all the better for being generous. Transfer the outline to the garden by using a spike to act as

SPECIAL FEATURE

❖

Why not build a seat of chamomile or thyme? Construct a raised bed 45cm (18in) high, with stone or brick sides. Fork over the bottom of the bed, put in a 15cm (6in) layer of broken stone or hardcore, top this with a layer of geo-textile membrane and fill with topsoil. Plant the top with small species at the recommended distance apart. Once established, the feature will look delightful and be fragrant in use.

a radius from which you swing a line to produce the finished curve.

LAWNS FOR PLAY

Grass is a soft surface and lawns were made for play, so make sure your lawn is of ample size and of a quality that will take regular cup finals and test matches. If turf was laid by a builder it will probably be fairly tough, with a proportion of hard-wearing rye grass; if you are seeding a lawn from scratch, make sure your seed mix includes rye grass.

◁ GRASS CAN CREATE a most interesting juxtaposition with paving slabs, in this case helping to break up the expanse of a path.

△ THERE IS NOTHING BETTER than a sweep of lawn to lead your eye around the garden. Generous curves make mowing easier.

PRACTICALITIES

Regular lawn maintenance is not onerous if you incorporate a number of features and factors to make life easier. The first is to keep the shape simple, so the area can be easily mown without having to back in and out of awkward corners. Edging by hand can be time-consuming, so consider laying a mowing edge (a paved strip set just below the turf – see inset) so the machine can run smoothly over the top.

This may take the form of a narrow path, laid as slabs or brick, to prevent border plants from flopping out on to the lawn, where they would also impede mowing.

Stepping stones across a lawn should also be set just below the turf level, as should an edge to a terrace or patio. If the terrace is raised, lay a mowing strip between the grass and the upstand so that the mower misses the raised area.

▷ A CURVED PATH around this garden is set into the lawn in the form of irregularly shaped stepping stones to prevent wear to the grass.

Paving and patios

Paved areas form a major part of the garden's hard landscaping and will take the lion's share of your budget, so their design and construction are crucial. Having hundreds of different paving materials and styles to choose from makes decisions difficult but remember that simplicity, and a visual link with the surroundings, are the keys to good design. Paving forms the background to a wide range of activities, such as outdoor eating, so it must be integrated into the garden, preferably through plants.

Random-sized cobbles

PAVED GARDENS

'Patio' is the correct name for a paved and walled garden, although the word is now used to describe any hard-surfaced area. There are certain situations, where space is limited or where grass is unnecessary, in which a completely paved area, together with planting at ground level or in raised beds or containers, will form the perfect courtyard garden. If you add a well-designed water feature, some overhead beams, a barbecue and built-in

furniture, you have an outside room of the highest order. Such gardens may be found at ground level, in town or country, or even perched high above the city as a stunning rooftop living space.

SITING A PATIO

Most people automatically think of siting a patio in the sun, which makes sense for many cooler climates. But shade is a vital element in gardens in those parts of the world where the sun rises high in the sky, with correspondingly soaring temperatures. It is important to be aware of the aspect of your garden so that you know where its sunny and shady areas fall throughout the day and can site your patio accordingly, perhaps to catch the evening sun. Consider whether you might need to screen a patio from the prevailing wind. It is usually best to select a position that has easy access from the house, perhaps adjacent to it. You may also be able to provide a secret sitting area, tucked away in a secluded corner of the garden, perhaps shaded by an arbour

◁ **COLOURED COBBLES** *lend themselves to being laid in intricate patterns to enliven a paved area. Pack them closely together to leave no gaps.*

smothered in fragrant climbers, enabling you to get away from the clamour of house and family for a while.

PAVING MATERIALS

Different materials bring varied qualities to a paved area. Look at the range of materials on offer at any garden centre and assess their relative costs. Always try to link paving materials with those used in the house or elsewhere in the garden. While a single surface may look bland, three or more will be too busy.

Brick

Brick paving is small-scale, providing an intimate, often mellow surface that can form an obvious link with an adjoining brick-built house if the same colour and texture of bricks are used. It acts as an excellent foil to another surface, such as pre-cast concrete slabs or natural stone, when used in panels or a 'grid'. To make an interesting surface when used on their own, bricks can be laid in a number of patterns that include stretcher bond (like bricks in a wall), herringbone, basketweave and soldier courses.

Bricks vary in durability and some are too soft for paving, so make sure

THE IDEAL SIZE

❖

There is nothing worse than a terrace or patio whose dimensions are mean and, as a general rule, you should think of building something no smaller than a good-sized room inside the house. A minimum size of 3.6m by 3.6m (12ft by 12ft) will allow for eating comfortably. Keep the design simple, with a geometric pattern close to the house and more fluid, rounded shapes further away. A patio built up from a series of overlapping rectangles might offer opportunities for incorporating raised beds, seating and possibly water and a barbecue.

◁ **GRANITE SETTS** *have a slightly irregular and textured surface, making them ideal for paths and drives where grip is important. They also make an excellent edging to contain gravel.*

those you choose are hard enough to withstand frosty conditions. Today a wide range of frostproof paving bricks is available in all colours and textures; to be sure of quality, visit a good builder's yard or landscape centre. Check with the supplier or scrape the surface with a hard object. If it flakes away, do not use the bricks as a paving material. Engineering bricks, although hard, are not ideal for paving as they are slippery when wet.

Stone

Natural stone is the most expensive material available but looks superb and will last a lifetime. Random rectangular slabs are best for a terrace but need skilled laying. Because such paving is often recycled

from old mill floors or pavements, make sure the slabs are as clean as possible and not impregnated with oil, which can sweat out in hot weather. The

thickness varies, so the base foundation will have to take account of this. When laying, start with a small 'keystone' and radiate the pattern outwards, staggering

Engineering bricks

Brick patterned paving slab

Irregular-shaped paving slab

Riven concrete paving slab

Stable pavers

Precast concrete paving slab

30

the joints so that no more than two slabs line up with each other. New stone paving, of uniform thickness, is available, but the cost is usually prohibitive.

Both natural stone and concrete slabs are available in broken form, which can be used to lay 'crazy paving'. Visually, this can be a busy and potentially messy pattern, hard to lay effectively, and it could conflict with the clean lines of an adjoining house. It looks better laid within a framework of bricks but is generally best used in an informal part of the garden.

Reconstituted stone and concrete

The widest range of paving is essentially pre-cast concrete slabs, of various finishes. Some are exceptionally good substitutes for natural stone, the original moulds being taken from the real thing, complete with chisel marks and surface

INCORPORATING PLANTS

When laying 'random' paving, leave out the odd slab and remove any underlying hardcore. Break up the ground below and fill with clean soil, then plant low-growing species such as helianthemum or thyme that will sprawl over the surrounding paving.

irregularities. Other slabs are sharply architectural, with a smooth surface and regular edges. Let your choice be influenced by the prevailing design style of the adjoining house or wider location. Regular architectural slabs would look out of place in front of a country cottage but second-hand natural weathered stone, or a good imitation, could be just right. Colour is an important consideration: while grey

and the pale stone hues are fine, the more garish colours tend to look out of place. Size is also variable: use paving units all the same size to form a grid or random sizes to create a staggered pattern.

Granite setts and cobbles

Granite setts are either brick-shaped (full sets) or cubed (half sets). They were originally used as street paving and form a slightly uneven surface, making them ideal for drives or as an edge 'trim' around trees or another feature, but unsuitable for a terrace where tables and chairs are used. They are expensive and extremely durable. They have to be professionally laid over consolidated hardcore on a mortar bed.

Cobbles are egg-shaped, water-worn stones in a wide range of sizes. Like setts, they can be laid in beautifully complex patterns, either in large areas for driveways or in a more intimate setting. There is a delightful fashion for creating floor pictures in cobbles of different colours, the only limitation being your imagination. Cobbles should be packed tightly together and laid on a bed of mortar over well-consolidated hardcore.

Decking

Raised wooden decks are becoming ever more popular as a flooring material: they are lightweight, warm underfoot, shed water easily and cover up ugly surfaces. They are especially suitable for roof gardens, where weight is a consideration, as they can be suspended from the edges over much, or all, of the area. It is important to ensure adequate

◁ **TIMBER DECKING MAKES** *a wonderfully versatile surface. It can be quickly constructed and fits easily into a wide range of situations.*

◁ **TILES ARE USED** *to create an imaginative floorscape on this roof terrace. Diagonal lines distract the eye from the squareness of the area.*

bed bricks on wet mortar and carefully point the joints with mortar afterwards, being careful not to dirty their surface.

Laying concrete block pavers

Block pavers are the size of bricks but made from concrete. Available in a range of colours, they are ideal for paving drives and other areas of hard wear; the whole area must be contained within a fixed edge, preferably of blocks set in concrete. A well-consolidated base of hardcore is essential and the blocks are butt-jointed on sand before being 'vibrated' into position with a hired plate vibrator. More sand is brushed into the surface and the area vibrated again.

ventilation below the deck to minimize rotting. The basic construction is much the same as a floor inside the house, the boards being nailed to joists which in turn are bolted to posts set in concrete. Use pressure-treated softwood or hardwood from a renewable source. The widths of the boards can be varied, to set up an interesting surface pattern, and stains in a wide range of colours can be used to link decking with a colour scheme on the exterior of the building or inside the home.

Decks are a useful solution on sloping sites where they can be built as a series of interlocking terraces, framed by railings or built-in seating and linked by steps.

LAYING PAVING

The unseen preparation is all-important to ensure a long and durable life; paving laid on poor foundations or with an uneven surface will quickly deteriorate and may become unsafe. Any paved area should finish below the damp-proof course of the house to prevent moisture working its way through the wall into your home. And give paving a slight

'fall' of not less than 1:100, to allow water to run away from the building.

The depth of foundations for paving will vary, depending on the type of ground. Remove all topsoil first as it is organic and can rot down over time, causing subsidence. Bearing in mind that the finished paving level should be 15cm (6in) below the damp-proof course, excavate to allow for a layer of well-compacted hardcore or crushed stone 10cm (4in) thick, topped with a layer of sharp sand and small stones (ballast) so that all gaps in the hardcore are filled in.

Laying brick pavers

Special paving bricks are about the thickness of a paving slab, but if you are using a conventional house brick for a paved area remember to adjust the foundation level accordingly. Lay bricks on a 5cm (2in) bed of semi-dry mortar, consisting of four parts soft sand to one part cement. Once the bricks are in position, brush more dry mortar into the joints and leave to set with the aid of water absorbed from the ground by capillary action. Alternatively you can

---

LAYING PAVING SLABS

❖

Prepare a good foundation and position each slab on five spots of mortar, one at each corner and one in the centre, then carefully tamp them down to achieve the right level. Slabs can either be butt-jointed, to fit tightly together, or laid with joints, using wooden spacers that are removed before pointing.

Designing with paths

While a patio or terrace is a static feature, paths provide movement, allowing access to all parts of the garden by taking the most interesting route around it. They define and often separate the major areas such as lawn, planting and utility. Not only practical, garden paths are a major design element that need to be sited carefully in relation to the overall layout.

32

Gravel

Ornamental stone chippings

△ **BRICK IS AN IDEAL** *material for paths in a traditional garden setting. Fringed by* Sedum spectabile, *this herringbone path has been softened by letting moss grow between the bricks.*

THE ROLE OF PATHS

While the prime function of a path is to take you from A to B, paths should also blend into the garden and may not necessarily take the most direct route. When working out a design, professionals refer to 'desire lines': these are the most logical, and often the shortest, route between two different points in the garden.

When you are formulating your garden plan, take account of where various features are positioned and link them with paths that take a pleasing and practical course through the garden. A vegetable garden or area for salad crops will need all-weather access from the kitchen rather than a tramp over a soggy lawn in the depth of winter. Similarly, to reach a shed set diagonally on the other side of the lawn from the back door, you might need to lay a line of carefully positioned stepping stones set into the lawn. And, leading up to a gate or an entrance, there should ideally be a path that

allows two people to pass each other easily. The width of a path is important. While stepping stones can be laid with a single row of paving slabs, a route that is regularly used by wheelbarrows and wheeled toys should be approximately 90cm (3ft) wide.

Besides fulfilling a practical role, paths should be given visual continuity with the rest of the garden. Try to use bricks or paving slabs similar to those laid in a terrace or patio.

▷ **REMEMBER THAT** *paths and paving should form a simple background and not detract from planting or other features on either side of them.*

◁ GRAVEL OFFERS
a neat, practical and low-cost surface that is ideal for paths and drives on a level site. As gravel is a mobile material, it needs to be given an edging, in this case of brick, to retain it.

gravel, small cobbles, bark chips and tarmac are fluid and can be more easily laid in sweeping curves and irregular shapes. Slabs, bricks and concrete blocks should be laid in exactly the same way as a terrace, over a well-consolidated base of hardcore.

Concrete

Concrete is the stone of the twentieth century, elegant and durable. It can be laid over a hardcore base and finished in numerous ways that will include trowelling smooth, tamping to formed a ribbed effect, 'seeding' with gravel when still wet, or brushing with a stiff or soft broom to produce yet more finishes.

Gravel

Gravel is an excellent low-cost material, both for an informal path and to create a flowing surface over a larger area. There are wide regional variations in colour and texture. The correct laying of gravel is crucial as thorough compaction is essential at all stages. It requires a well-consolidated hardcore base not less than 10cm (4in) thick, topped with a 5cm (2in) layer of coarse gravel, again well compacted. Finish with a 2.5cm (1in) layer of fine gravel mixed with 'hoggin', which is a clay binder, usually from the same gravel pit. Roll a final, thin top-dressing of washed shingle into the hoggin to finish the job neatly. Gravel drives should have a camber to shed water easily and all gravel surfaces need 'edge restraints', which could be bricks set in concrete, or boards pegged firmly in place, to stop it spreading everywhere.

STEPPING STONES

❖

When laying stepping stones across a lawn, position them on the turf and walk over them to get the spacing right. Leave slabs in place, cut round them with a sharp spade, remove the turf and bed the slabs on a weak concrete mix so the finished level is just below the lawn.

Log slices, 15cm (6in) thick, make an excellent woodland or informal path through planting. In a shady area, staple chicken wire to their surface to provide added grip.

▷ **THIS PATH** *running through a lawn is made up of setts. They have been bedded on the soil, just below the level of the grass, so that a mower can run smoothly over the top.*

SHAPES AND MATERIALS

While a straight path looks fine in a formal layout, it naturally encourages faster movement than a route which gently meanders, perhaps disappearing from view with a feeling of mystery. The materials you choose and the way in which you lay them will also have a visual impact. Slabs or bricks laid in a staggered bond down the length of a path tend to lead the eye on, encouraging movement, whereas the same materials laid across the path slow things down visually.

Bricks and slabs are 'modular' materials, having a fixed size and lending themselves to rectangular paving patterns, but surfaces like

Changes of level

Sloping gardens can often provide greater interest than a flat plot, as areas created at different levels may become individual spaces with their own theme. Such spaces will need to be linked with the rest of the garden in some way, either by the inclusion of steps or by making a ramp, both of which can become important features in their own right.

34

INTEGRATING STEPS

The design of steps should always take its cue from the immediate surroundings. If you are stepping down from a terrace precisely laid with brick or with pre-cast slabs, use similar materials for the steps. If, on the other hand, the change of level is some way from the house, in an informal part of the garden, the steps can be built from logs, railway sleepers or natural stone, to reflect this. As a general rule, it is a good idea to keep to a more 'architectural' treatment close to the house and more informal further away. A change of level also offers the opportunity to incorporate other features, such as a well-planned rocky outcrop, or a series of pools that drops down the slope, in association with the steps. Steps need not necessarily occupy only one part of the garden; if you make them large enough – big circles or overlapping hexagons, for example – they become more like a series of terraces and could form virtually the whole of a sloping site. If you make the edge or outline of brick or stone, the 'treads' forming the main garden areas could be laid with paving of various kinds or with gravel, grass or even planting.

STEPS: THE PRACTICALITIES

Make steps as broad and generous as possible as there is nothing worse – or more dangerous – than a mean and narrow flight. It is important to get the proportions right, both visually and for comfort: each step should have a 'rise' of 15cm (6in) and a tread of 45cm (18in).

◁ **IN AN INFORMAL SITUATION,** *planting can be introduced to soften the line of steps.*

There are no set rules about their width, but a wide flight looks more restful, and will be easier to negotiate than a narrow one. In a long flight of steps, you might incorporate a landing every 10–15 treads: this could provide a platform for a group of pots or other garden ornaments. Remember that steps need not necessarily go straight up a slope; they could change direction to take a zig-zag course up a steep change of level.

The construction of steps up a shallow slope can become a straightforward DIY project; if you use logs or railway sleepers, these are simply pegged firmly into the slope. But steep changes in level and complex step structures will need specialist input in terms of both building and their design. Always seek professional help if you are in any doubt at all.

Steps can be built from virtually any of the usual hard landscape materials; where stone or pre-cast concrete slabs are used for the treads, let them overhang the risers by just under 5cm (2in) to create a discreet shadow line that will visually soften the flight. In

◁ **BRICKWORK PROVIDES** *continuity* (far left) *between the raised beds and the wide flight of steps.*

A CO-ORDINATING PAINT SCHEME *and crisp detailing* (left) *tie in these wooden steps with the decking and balustrades in a contemporary garden on two levels.*

△ **A TIMBER EDGING** *perfectly integrates these brick steps with the built-in raised beds from which planting cascades from level to level.*

order to emphasize a change of level from terrace to steps, lay a course of bricks, or other contrasting material, flush with the edge of the paving. This gives an indication of the position of the first step to someone who is unfamiliar with the garden layout.

MAKING A RAMP

If steps were used to link every level in a garden, it would be virtually impossible to move mowers, barrows, wheelchairs or wheeled toys from place to place. To give easy access for wheeled vehicles and for elderly or disabled gardeners or visitors, it makes sense to incorporate a ramp, or a series

of slopes. Be sure you have enough space: a comfortable gradient of 1:25 or 1:50 makes a ramp two to three times the length of a flight of steps.

RAISED BEDS

While raised beds can be a freestanding feature within a paved area or other area of the garden, they can also become part of a flight of steps or change of level. If they are also helping to retain the slope, they should be built with this in mind, with suitable drainage incorporated at regular intervals. Since the walls of built-in raised beds have to take pressure, it is advisable to seek professional advice for any such wall over 60cm (2ft) high.

Freestanding raised beds can be rectangular or curved; always design them to fit in with the surroundings or underlying paving pattern. The walls

---

STEP SAFETY

Both steps and ramps should be lit for safety at night. The neatest solution is to build lighting into the flanking walls or the step risers, otherwise you can position low-level lights to flank a flight of steps. If there is a steep drop, or if elderly people will use the garden, it is a good idea to incorporate a handrail too: make sure it is sturdy.

---

can be built from virtually any material, as well as timber and railway sleepers. Their construction is similar to that of boundary walls, with a suitable concrete foundation and a coping at the top. A height of about 45cm (18in) will allow the wall of the raised bed to double as an occasional seat.

Fork over the bottom of the raised bed and fill it with approximately 15cm (6in) of clean hardcore. Top this with a layer of geo-textile membrane (available at your local garden centre) and fill the bed up with clean topsoil.

△ **RAILWAY SLEEPERS** *make ideal shallow steps for an informal part of the garden. The repetition of pots emphasizes the rhythm of the flight.*

Arches, arbours and pergolas

Garden features such as arches and pergolas bring a vertical dimension to the garden and often act as a major focal point. As well as drawing the eye they can also be invaluable for providing shade or screening a bad view; they act as hosts for climbing plants too.

36

THE ROLE OF VERTICAL FEATURES

Both arches and pergolas encourage movement through the garden. Arches are usually set over a gateway or entrance and serve as an entry point into the garden or into one area of it from another, or they can be positioned as a focal point, flanked by trellis, planting or hedges that separate different garden areas. Pergolas are like a series of arches joined together to form a single structure, providing a linking element that leads you from one distinct point to another. They often span a paved path, though the ground-level surface may well be grass. Arches induce a feeling of tension as you approach them, coupled with that essential element of mystery as you try to glimpse what is beyond.

Pergolas, while also creating tension, draw you into a soft, green tunnel of flower and foliage, dappled with sunlight and allowing tantalizing views of the garden to either side, framed by the upright posts. Part of the essential function of a pergola is that it leads to somewhere positive, which might be another part of the garden or a well-positioned focal point or seat; it should not simply lead to the incinerator or the compost heap!

An arbour, on the other hand, is a static feature. It is an open-sided structure, usually set over a quiet sitting area and often situated in an informal part of the garden. Arbours can also be smothered with climbers, which should preferably be fragrant.

Another feature, sometimes erroneously called a pergola, uses an open framework of overhead beams built out from the house or a wall. It is often positioned directly above a patio, where it will cast light shade when covered with climbing plants, and will also be useful for masking a view from neighbouring windows.

A HARMONIOUS DESIGN

The design of arches, pergolas and arbours should be in keeping with the overall style of the garden and their position within it. Close to the house the design might be crisply architectural, constructed from planed timber or metal hoops. In a more distant part of a garden the character could be distinctly informal, using piers of old brick and cross-beams of solid

△ **A SQUARE-TOPPED ARCH** *provides support for Rosa 'Albertine'. Timber is easy to work with and offers versatility, ideal for a do-it-yourself project.*

△ **ARCHES AND ENTRANCES** *provide the classic garden elements of tension, mystery and surprise. This brick-built arch is covered by honeysuckle to entice the visitor with its fragrance.*

◁ **A PERGOLA** *should always have a positive focus, the hoops of this stained timber tunnel drawing the eye along to the handsome urn at its end. Roses and wisteria provide a charming plant combination trained up the sides and over the arched top, casting dappled shade below.*

WHICH CLIMBERS?

Climbers grown over a freestanding structure often do better than when planted against a wall or fence because they receive plenty of light and moisture. If an arch or pergola is of ample size, virtually any climbing plant will be suitable, but if the gap is narrow you should avoid roses with sharp thorns, or other bushy plants. While the choice of a single species can be fine, a combination of climbers would extend the flowering season and provide an attractive mix. You might grow laburnum, trained over the structure, together with wisteria or the large-leafed vine *Vitis coignetiae* with the late-flowering *Clematis tangutica*. For fragrance, think of planting summer jasmine, honeysuckle or scented roses.

timber. It is important that these features are simply designed, in proportions that are as bold and generous as possible, and they should be amply planted. Flimsy metal and timber structures will deteriorate quickly and can look appalling. Each of these vertical features is one of the easier garden projects to build yourself: for inspiration, look at traditional designs in many older gardens.

If bought off the peg, these garden features are usually easy enough to assemble by slotting components together and fixing them into spiked metal sockets driven into the ground or concreting posts into position. Timber posts will generally have been pressure-treated to prevent rot, but it will be

worth applying additional non-toxic preservative every two or three years; bear in mind that climbers will have to be taken down in order to do this, however. Metal hoops are usually plastic-coated and will need little maintenance. You could paint or stain a pergola or arch to match with a colour scheme used elsewhere in the garden; paints and stains formulated for outdoor woodwork come in a wide range of colours; shades of blue and green blend into the garden but primary colours can have a bold impact.

▷ **SHADE IS IMPORTANT** *in a garden and may have to be created. Here, vine-covered overhead beams built out from a boundary and supported by wooden posts make a sheltered sitting area.*

Screens within the garden

A garden that can be divided into separate areas, perhaps having their own theme, will always be more interesting than a space that can be taken in at a single glance. The way in which you divide a garden depends on its size and shape as well as the budget available. Solid divisions can be created by a wall or hedge or can be more minimal, using trellis screens or a limited number of well-chosen shrubs. Sensitive manipulation of the space can help you to introduce the elements of mystery and surprise.

38

△ SCREENS NEED
NOT *be expensive
and a little
imagination can
work wonders. This
simple bamboo blind
provides privacy by
hiding the house and
garden behind.*

OUTDOOR ROOMS

If you have taken over an established garden, the bones of internal divisions may already exist or they can be strengthened to break your view from one area through to another. An existing 'wing' of planting to one side of a plot could be echoed by a new bed, either directly opposite, to achieve a balanced and formal effect, or offset, to create a more informal sense. Hedges, on the other hand, will have a far more architectural feel and can be clipped either to form a simple rectangular outline or with their ends curved down. If a hedge is set within a bed, allow

room for clipping by laying a simple path with slabs or stepping stones to either side.

Trellis is a favourite divider, but instead of buying standard panels from a garden centre, why not think of making your own, taking your inspiration from screens created by interior designers? You will see endless variations in restaurants and other public places that use different patterns, widths of timber and colours, all of which could be adapted for outdoor use. At the end of a run of trellis you might position a timber obelisk that will provide a positive full stop or focal point.

Slim vertical slats set between a top and bottom rail will form a delicate wooden screen, as will bamboo poles, perhaps with the tops at slightly different heights to set up a fascinating rhythm.

SOLID SCREENS

Walls are the most expensive option and make an opaque screen; always use walling materials that link with the house or other features. A solid wall can create a good deal of turbulence on the lee side of it, however, whereas a

▽ HEDGES ARE A
*versatile living screen
and most species
develop rapidly in
well-prepared soil.
This hedge of purple-
leaved prunus
encloses an intimate
garden room.*

BUDGET OPTIONS

The cheapest screen is created by using a few well-chosen plants that simply break your line of vision. If a path curves away past this it will naturally encourage a sense of movement and some expectation as to just what lies beyond. You can make an elegant and attractive screen by constructing a timber frame of top and bottom rails, approximately 1.8m (6ft) high, and stretching vertical wires between them. The wires will act as a host to climbing plants and soften your screen with vegetation.

△ OUT OF SIGHT . . . *A well-positioned shrub provides a simple but effective screen to this compost heap.*

▷ TRELLIS CAN BE BOUGHT *in a wide range of patterns. In this garden the sturdy trellis with elaborate finials makes a handsome feature as well as an ideal host for climbing plants. You could design and make your own panels, which will be cheaper as well as more original.*

screen that is pierced or has gaps in it makes a far better windbreak because it filters the flow of air, rather than blocking it. One such screen is the 'honeycomb' brick wall in which gaps are left between every other brick so that you catch a glimpse of what lies beyond the wall.

Focal points

Focal points are the exclamation marks of a garden – they draw the eye, bringing surprise and adding interest. The primary rule is to choose and use them sparingly: too many will over-complicate a design but one or two, carefully positioned, will give it a focus. Make sure that not more than one focal point is visible at any one time, otherwise your eye will be diverted from one place to another, weakening their impact.

40

△ LOOKING GOOD *at all times of year, this pale bust stands out in sharp relief against the dark background of yew. It is surrounded in winter by the frosted spikes of rosemary.*

▽ A STRONG EYE-CATCHER, *like this urn mounted on a stone plinth, needs to be positioned with care: if it is too dominant, it could foreshorten a view.*

THE CHOICE

The choice of a focal point will be up to you but it should be something that commands attention. In a small garden it might be a large container, an urn or a sculpted figure, perhaps placed at the end of a pergola, or positioned to draw the eye diagonally across a lawn, helping to open up the space. It might be a sculptural group of plants, a flowering tree against an undemanding background or the simple plume of a fountain set in the middle of a circular lawn. Larger focal points could take the form of a summer house or gazebo, a rock outcrop or a major water feature.

As any such element, large or small, is an attractive part of the garden, you are naturally drawn to walk towards it. Once there, you are bound to turn round and take in the reverse view, which you should ensure is equally pleasing; there will be little point in looking at the back of someone's garage or an unsightly building.

Apart from containers, sculpture and statuary that can be bought off the shelf, do not ignore the potential charm and eye-catching qualities of found objects. These are generally more personal and might include a gnarled log set beside an informal path or a piece of sun-bleached driftwood on an architectural terrace. Groups of smooth stones or boulders can be carefully placed to draw the eye and topiary, strategically positioned, will provide interest throughout the year. All such *objets trouvés* will cost you virtually nothing but they can add immeasurably to the overall design of the garden.

FORMAL OR INFORMAL?

As a general rule, classical urns, bowls and statues will sit most comfortably in a formal layout and should be placed geometrically on one of the garden's main axes. Planted containers and all kinds of found object, on the other hand, make useful focal points in a more informal or free-flowing layout.

◁ FOCAL POINTS *can be practical too and a number of obelisks could be placed around a potager to host runner beans. If you want to make them even more eye-catching, you could always paint them.*

Sometimes the degree of formality lies mainly in the materials: a stone obelisk will demand attention in an architectural setting, while a similar feature made from trellis and smothered in plants makes an altogether softer outline, or that which is more appropriate in an informal setting.

FOCAL POINTS IN SMALL GARDENS

In small gardens, the choice of focal points has to be carefully controlled, otherwise the garden will become hopelessly busy. Much has to do with compatibility and in a small town garden a collection of terracotta containers at the foot of a wall might form a composition that is sufficiently unified to serve as a focal point. Always remember the precept 'less is more' in a small space and be sparing in your choice. At the same time you should not be afraid to ring the changes by moving ornaments or other focal points around, in much the same way as you might do inside the house.

Painted scenes on the walls of a small garden can be both humorous and exotic and they certainly draw the eye. You might paint a false doorway, slightly ajar to give a glimpse of an imaginary landscape beyond. Mirrors can also be an invaluable way of drawing the eye at the same time as increasing the feeling of space; be sure not to position them at the end of a path or you will simply see yourself approaching and there will be no sense of mystery. Angling a mirror into planting, so that it appears to recede into the distance, is generally a much better solution.

△ GENEROUS-SIZED CONTAINERS, *like this olive jar, always draw the eye and often look far better left unplanted. Set them among foliage which will enhance and just temper their architectural line.*

Pools and other water features

Water is one of the most attractive elements in any garden, bringing movement and sound as well as being a cooling influence and a haven for many kinds of wildlife. Water features can be large or small, formal or informal and, with most garden centres selling a huge range of equipment and suitable plants, there should be something to suit all tastes and type of plot.

42

△ **THE CLASSIC** *garden elements of paving, planting and water are perfectly combined in this simple but striking geometric design.*

FORMAL OR INFORMAL?

Water features divide quite clearly into the formal and the informal and your choice will be influenced by the feature's position within the garden and, of course, by the character of the garden design. In general terms the areas closer to the house will be planned in a more architectural way, very often with a crisp paving pattern based on a series of overlapping rectangles. A geometric-shaped pool will fit readily into this pattern. In a totally formal garden you might have a pair of rectangular or square pools balancing each other on opposite sides of a courtyard garden.

In the more distant parts of a garden, where the design can be less formal, using strong, flowing curves, the water feature can take a more informal outline. Taking this to the extreme, you could create a natural wildlife pool, flanked by marginal and bog planting and set within gently undulating ground.

Naturally sloping ground may provide the perfect opportunity for a series of pools set one above the other, with a linking stream or cascade; this could be designed in either a formal or an informal way, to match the style of garden.

▷ **THE CRISP FORMALITY** *of this pool is echoed by the symmetrical placing of iris and water lilies. Raising the feature slightly gives it greater importance, allowing the outline to stand out in sharp relief.*

△ **AN INFORMAL POOL** *needs balanced planting to attract wildlife. A pebble beach will allow birds, frogs and many other creatures to visit the pool.*

43

∇ **WATER CAN PROVIDE** *movement, sound and interest in even the smallest garden. Here, a water feature on two levels allows the fish to gush water into a pool below.*

SUNKEN OR RAISED?

The question of whether water should be set at, or above, ground level will depend on the character of the surrounding area. While a raised pool, its sides crisply constructed from bricks or stone, may be the perfect complement to a formal terrace, such a feature would look out of place in the further reaches of a garden, which is altogether less formal; in this case a free-form shape, flush with the ground, may be called for.

A raised pool should always look comfortable: if built too high, it will simply look incongruous. A good height is 45cm (18in), which allows people to sit on the edge, doubling as an occasional seat. A raised pool may well have started life as something else; for safety reasons, open water in the garden is not a good idea while toddlers are growing up, but a raised bed or a sandpit could easily be converted to water at a later date.

WILDLIFE POOLS

In reality, any body of water will encourage wildlife and even a formal pool will be attractive to a range of species from fish and aquatic plants to all kinds of insects, frogs and toads as well as visitors such as birds. Most people's perception of a wildlife pool, however, is an informal pond, set some way from the house (though not in shade). Planting can and should be incorporated both in the water itself and around the margins; the pool could also include a boggy area which in turn leads into drier shrub and mixed planting. In this way you will offer a wide range of habitats for wildlife and if you can also provide a log pile, leaf litter and a nearby hedge, so much the better. Beauty is always in the eye of the beholder and such an area should be truly informal, rather than a mess, so do not be tempted to clean it up too often or you may well damage sensitive ecosystems.

44 BOG GARDENS

There are many superb plants that grow naturally in the marshy or boggy conditions that occur around a natural pool. Many of these have handsome foliage and striking flowers. In an artificial situation you will have to create a boggy area and this can be done by allowing water to seep over the edge of a pool constructed from a pond liner, into another lined area that is filled with soil. The liner must be perforated to prevent the garden from becoming waterlogged.

MOVING WATER

While a still sheet of water can set up wonderful reflections, movement will bring a new dimension to the garden. Moving water will also provide a degree of aeration that is beneficial for fish, particularly during hot summer days. There are numerous ways in which you can introduce moving water, from a simple bubble jet set in the middle of a small pool to the most elaborate fountains, cascades and water slides, but the golden rule is to keep things simple.

Moving water features divide into the informality of natural streams and cascades and more formal jets and fountains. Position them appropriately within the overall garden layout. There is a wide range of perfectly safe submersible pumps to drive the largest waterfall or the smallest bubble jet. Exceptionally durable, pumps can be bought at any good garden centre or nursery that specializes in water gardening; they will also advise you on the correct size of pump for the water feature in question.

SMALL WATER FEATURES

Even the smallest patio or courtyard can incorporate a water feature, ranging from a 'millstone' with water flowing over its surface, to a classical mask that spouts into a trough below. Most such water features are positioned over a concealed sump, where a submersible small pump recirculates water around the system. The advantage of millstones, or features where water cascades out of a container into a bed of stones or cobbles, is that they are far safer for young children than an open stretch of water. Many such features can be bought off the peg or, with a little imagination and practical know-how, can be constructed as a uniquely personal focal point.

◁ IN A SLOPING GARDEN *the possibilities for creating streams, cascades and pools are endless. Hostas and salix, seen here, are among the many plants that will thrive in damp soils.*

△ THERE IS NO NEED FOR A FOUNTAIN *to create interest in a tiny garden: a simple mask and spout pouring water into a brimming stone tank bring all the soothing qualities of water.*

PRACTICALITIES

The success of a pool lies in getting the right balance of wildlife; this includes plants as well as fish and a myriad other tiny creatures that will be drawn to the pool. This means that, within reason, the larger the pool the better; it will certainly be difficult to achieve a balanced ecosystem in a pool that is less than 1.8m (6ft) square. Depth is another important consideration, as is the shape below the water level, known as the profile. While a garden pool need be no more than 45cm (18in) deep, it should include a 'marginal shelf', extending around approximately two-thirds of the pool; this will allow you to grow aquatic plants that enjoy just having their toes in the water. The shelf should be about 22cm (9in) below the water level; if it is built in two sections, bays will be left that form ideal breeding areas for fish.

A pond or pool should always be positioned in an open situation, away from deep shade or overhanging trees. Neither fish nor aquatic plants will thrive in total shade and fish can be harmed by dead leaves or other vegetation falling into the water and rotting.

CONSTRUCTION OPTIONS

In recent years the use of plastics and glass fibre has transformed pool construction into an easy, home-build option. The real choice is between a rigid, preformed pool and one that uses a 'liner' of some kind. Preformed pools are easy to install but can only be bought in a limited range of sizes, mostly small. They are simply bedded on sand in a suitable excavation; always make sure that the rim is absolutely level by using a long straightedge and a spirit level.

Larger pools can be constructed using a tough liner made of laminated PVC or butyl rubber. Liners can be bought from any good garden centre; they come with full instructions for their installation. Since liners can easily be punctured by sharp stones, their excavation must take this into account and the liner should be bedded on a 5cm (2in) layer of sand. The 'profile' of the pool excavation should include marginal shelves and the liner can be continued to form a bog garden around part of the perimeter.

Water features involving streams and changes of level are more difficult to construct yourself and may well need to be left in the hands of a professional with the necessary expertise and equipment. Such features will almost certainly use submersible pumps and may also need a filtration unit.

WATER SAFETY

❖

- An open body of water is dangerous for young children, so always bear this in mind when choosing and siting any feature.

- Electricity is potentially lethal and, although most water-feature kits are easy to use and install, make sure you follow the instructions and safety codes to the letter.

- All pumps are completely sealed and many run off a 12-volt power supply through a transformer safety device that will automatically switch off the system in the event of failure.

- There is a wide range of exterior light and power fittings designed for safe garden use.

- If in any doubt about anything electrical in the garden, be sure to enlist the help of a qualified electrician.

45

△ IF YOU HAVE *young children and are worried about open water in the garden, build something entirely safe that recirculates water from a concealed sump, through a pot or similar feature.*

Garden buildings

Your garden is both a practical and a decorative space and has to cater for a wide range of activities as well as storage. It is inevitable that you will have to find room for at least one utilitarian building, but with a little imagination and modification these can be dressed up, camouflaged or screened, or built from scratch and integrated as an attractive feature of the design.

46

△ **WITH CAREFUL ORGANIZATION** *you can grow a surprising amount in a tiny greenhouse.*

SHEDS

With houses on the whole becoming smaller and more cars standing on the drive, there is usually a real need to provide storage space in the garden. At the very least this will be needed for garden tools and equipment, but it often has to cater also for children's bikes and outdoor toys as well as garden furniture. A good-sized shed is usually the answer and it is generally good advice to buy one that is large rather than small for your immediate needs. Durability is also important: make sure the building is constructed from good quality timber and is soundly put together. You can then either hide the shed from view or dress it up to make it look more attractive.

As an alternative you can construct your own shed, tailoring it to your needs exactly, making it either free-standing or a lean-to structure against a wall. To prevent rot, always stand a building on a firm, dry base which can either be concrete, paving slabs or well-laid gravel. Since the roof will have the potential to collect rainwater, always fit a gutter and run this via a downpipe into a water butt.

GREENHOUSES

Make sure that a greenhouse, like a shed, is big enough for your needs. Many people who start off with a small glasshouse soon get the bug for growing exotic plants or raising seeds and wish they had bought a bigger model. Position a greenhouse in an open position that receives plenty of sun throughout the day. If you are considering using a propagator or electric heater, it will be essential to have a safe supply of electricity laid on by a qualified electrician.

Greenhouses can be made of metal (usually aluminium), which has a longer, maintenance-free life, or timber, which is traditional and blends into the garden well but which needs regular applications of a non-toxic preservative. They may be glazed down to the ground or have brick sides a third of the way up. Greenhouse bases usually come as pre-cast concrete strips and the floor can either be solid

throughout or have earth beds on either side for cultivation, with a central path.

SUMMER HOUSES

These are simply small garden buildings designed for leisure. They will inevitably become a focal point of the garden and should be carefully positioned to draw the eye in a particular direction. Remember that when you are sitting in or outside the building, the view back from the summer house is equally important, so make sure it has a pleasing prospect. There is a wide range of different styles of building available, but bear in mind that the summer house should be in keeping with the rest of the garden and the adjoining house. You would not put a rustic, timbered summer house alongside a crisp glass and concrete building, for example. A simple design will look comfortable in most garden surroundings.

◁ **THIS PAN-TILED** *shed is pretty enough to suit any traditional garden. It is partially screened by roses 'Mme. Plantier' and 'New Dawn' smothering the wall.*

TONING DOWN NEW BUILDINGS

❖

Many new timber buildings look garish and stark when new, standing out like a sore thumb. If you tone them down with a suitable shade of non-toxic preservative, or even a wood stain, they will settle far more comfortably and discreetly into their outdoor surroundings.

◁ A SUMMER HOUSE CAN *fulfil several roles in a small town garden. This one acts as a focal point, offering a shady place to sit while helping to screen the adjoining buildings from view.*

∇ THIS WOODEN GAZEBO *acts a a linking element and offers views into two garden rooms. The blue woodwork makes a bold statement and serves as a host to* Rosa 'Aloha'.

INTEGRATION AND ACCESS

Any garden building should be integrated into the design in its initial stages, which really comes down to sensible planning. If space permits, it makes sense to incorporate a hard-surfaced work area into the garden that could accommodate shed, greenhouse, incinerator and compost bins. It could be neatly screened off from the rest of the garden but linked to the house, or other parts of the garden, by means of a path or other paving. A summer house, being a fair-weather building, could simply sit on the far side of a lawn, where it would act as a large-scale focal point; it need not necessarily have a direct path leading to it.

Garden security

Garden security is becoming increasingly important, not just as a deterrent for house burglary but also against the theft of ornaments and features from the garden itself. There are many ways in which intruders can be discouraged and the methods should always be as unobtrusive as possible, for both practical and aesthetic reasons.

48

▽ **LIGHTING CAN** *be both practical and good-looking. These simple glass globes make a positive contribution to this small garden.*

LIGHTING

Garden lighting can serve either a practical or a decorative purpose, although there is considerable overlap between the two roles. On a practical level, garden lights are used to illuminate entrances, driveways, paths, patios, steps and general areas around the house and garden buildings. All too often such lighting is provided by extremely bright halogen floodlights, which are surrounded by deep pools of shadow in which people are practically invisible. Security lighting is often far more effective, using a lower-powered light with a more diffused beam so that pools of illumination merge together. The effect created also looks much less harsh.

△ **SPIKY AND THORNY** *plants on a boundary provide a real deterrent to intruders. This holly (Ilex aquifolium 'Argentea Marginata') is a superb evergreen for year-round interest.*

EFFECTIVE SOLUTIONS

Lighting along a drive needs to be both effective and aesthetically pleasing at the same time. Avoid the ostentation of imitation 'street lamps' up the drive and instead use lower-level fittings that can cast light across the surface of the drive or path. The pupose is to illuminate where you are going, not the top of your head. Exactly the same principle applies to lighting steps: special fittings can either be built into the risers, so that light is cast directly onto the treads, or well designed fittings positioned to either side of the flight.

There are many forms of decorative outdoor lighting, varying in sophistication from easily installed, low-voltage kits that you can position

△ **SURFACES THAT CRUNCH** *underfoot can be a surprisingly effective burglar deterrent and gravel is an ideal material in this respect for both paths and drives. Even if the crunch of an intruder is not immediately heard by people, it quickly attracts the attention of a dog.*

yourself to sophisticated schemes planned by a professional lighting installation company. Techniques such as floodlighting, spotlighting and backlighting are fairly obvious, but try moonlighting, where a light is suspended in the branches of a tree to cast delicate shadows on the ground, or 'grazing', where the beam is shone directly up or down a wall or other feature, picking out its surface pattern and texture.

BOUNDARIES AND PLANTING

Keeping your boundaries in good condition is an essential aspect of garden maintenance. Whereas a sound fence, whose gates are securely locked or bolted, will deter the casual thief, a broken one might do just the opposite. The type of boundary obviously comes into it too and you may have to decide between a low boundary that embraces a view and something higher that provides a physical barrier. This may be a situation where an electronic alarm could be used, but their installation is a specialist business if they are not to be continually tripped by passing animals.

Do not under-estimate the deterrent value of spiky, thorny or really dense planting, especially on the boundaries. A hedge of mature holly can provide a prickly formal boundary or you could equally well plan an informal border to include thorny shrubs like pyracantha, berberis, crataegus and mahonia, as well as yucca and other 'aggressive' species. The effect works both ways, however, and stout clothes and gloves will be needed for maintenance.

Planning the planting

While the hard landscape forms the 'bones' of a garden, it will be the plants that bring it to life with their ability to provide colour and interest throughout the year. It is worth taking your time over this stage, planning out the planting as an integrated exercise rather than simply plonking the

50

plants down in a random selection. Do some homework, check just how large each plant will get, whether it is evergreen or deciduous and when it flowers. Match up the needs of plants to the sunny and shady areas of your garden, the direction of a prevailing wind and, of course, whether your soil is acid or alkaline.

△ FRUIT TREES
*give an added bonus
to the spring garden
with their blossom.
This Japanese cherry
looks magnificent in
an informal part of
the garden, with a
carpet of bluebells at
ground level.*

THE STARTING POINT

Any garden is a contrived environment, but if we look at the way plants are grouped in the wild it will give us some good clues as to just where to start. A typical example is a rich, woodland habitat where the trees form the highest canopy, with a middle storey of indigenous shrub planting and a final, sprawling layer of ground cover. These same layers make perfect sense in a garden too, albeit usually in a more controlled and decorative way, and we will look at the different layers separately.

When putting a planting together, as a general rule it is far better to have well-stocked borders than a sea of soil with one or two sparse shrubs; apart from visual considerations, areas of bare soil offer rich potential for weed growth. It is also worth remembering that a greater number of plants, laid out in groups and drifts rather than as single specimens, will often reduce maintenance by knitting together as ground cover.

TREES

Trees are the giants of both the plant world and the garden, so it is important to choose the right ones. While a large garden may well have room for forest species such as oak, ash, lime or chestnut, the smaller garden would be quickly swamped by these. In this situation do your homework and choose smaller trees and position them carefully to draw the eye, provide

▽ IN THIS SHADY
CORNER *viburnum,
laurel, ornamental
maple, hostas and
day lilies create a
tiered effect, their
yellow flowers and
foliage bringing the
border to life.*

screening and create high-level interest without casting shadow in the wrong place. A good choice might include silver birch, sorbus, crab apple (*Malus*) and the smaller flowering cherries (*Prunus*). Do not be seduced into planting weeping willows in small front gardens: they will quickly dwarf the house, if not the whole street. It makes sense not to plant a tree closer to the house than its eventual height, and never to plant water-demanding species such as poplar or willow close to a building, as subsidence could be a problem in certain types of soil.

When planting trees, always make sure they are firmly supported by a stout stake and the correct ties. Support is important during the early years so that the root system can develop as quickly as possible. Never use a bamboo cane as support or a pair of old tights or wire to secure a tree. Rubber tree ties can be bought from good garden centres.

ESTABLISHING THE FRAMEWORK

Most gardens will need a framework of tough, largely evergreen shrubs to wrap the space about, provide shelter from wind and possibly screen bad views, as well as providing a backdrop for more colourful material. In a small garden you would plant in groups of twos or threes, possibly even singles, but in a larger space the numbers could be correspondingly higher. Evergreen species such as bamboo, elaeagnus, laurel, mahonia, *Fatsia japonica*, *Viburnum rhytidophyllum* and *Choisya ternata* would be ideal.

△ **IN A SMALL TOWN GARDEN** *densely planted borders help to create a sense of privacy and to screen neighbouring views. A good proportion of evergreen framework plants ensures that there is interest in winter too.*

PLACING CONIFERS

❖

Conifers are the 'punctuation marks' of a planting scheme, drawing the eye and demanding attention. Use them sparingly and in specific places. Too many will produce a busy scheme as the eye darts about the garden from one to another. If you enjoy these beautiful plants, then group them together as a collection so that you can see the subtle variations in form and texture.

52

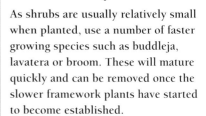

FAST-MATURING SHRUBS
❖

As shrubs are usually relatively small when planted, use a number of faster growing species such as buddleja, lavatera or broom. These will mature quickly and can be removed once the slower framework plants have started to become established.

Much framework planting will be set against a boundary and it is worth remembering that large, bold leaves tend to draw the eye and diminish the space – something to avoid on a fence or wall close to the house. Fine, feathery foliage, on the other hand, has just the opposite effect and can help to make a boundary recede visually.

FILLING IN

Once the framework is in position you can begin to fill in with lower, more colourful material. This should be a combination of shrubs and herbaceous planting, the shrubs providing structure and support to the herbaceous perennials, which will in turn give the necessary colour and delicacy. Numbers in a group or drift of plants can be greater than the background framework and should reinforce a sweeping curve or soften a sharp angle by using the same material on either side to lead the eye past.

THE GROUND FLOOR

At the lowest level, towards the front of a border, ground cover can be used in still greater numbers to create a carpet, link the various taller plants together and provide visual continuity. Such planting is usually permanent, using low-growing shrubs or hardy perennials, but annual

 THE COMBINATION
of different heights, colours and leaf textures produces an interesting and well-balanced border. The plants descend in tiered heights from the tall yellow spires of golden rod (Solidago) and the flat heads of achillea to the low-growing ground cover provided by geraniums and Stachys byzantina at the front of the border.

GOOD INFILL PLANTS
❖

Acanthus

Cytisus

Cistus

Delphiniums

Deutzia

Hydrangea

Lupins

Potentilla

Rosemary

Roses

Rudbeckia

Spiraea

GOOD GROUND FLOOR PLANTS
❖

Alchemilla

Bergenia

Cistus x dansereaui

Cotoneaster dammeri

Epimedium

Hebe pinguifolia

Hedera (ivy)

Hypericum calycinum

Geraniums

Lamium

Pachysandra

Vinca

plants can be very effective on a temporary basis, particularly when a border is developing and needs bulking up with instant flower and foliage.

When planting a border and grading it from taller plants at the back to lower-growing species towards the front, you can always add interest by drifting a number of taller species forward into the middle ground. This applies particularly to lofty hardy perennials such as delphiniums and lupins.

Spring bulbs and low-growing annuals, including half-hardy summer bedding, may be classed as ground cover and they can be invaluable in providing instant colour at different times of year, as well as for filling in gaps between slower-growing plants in a developing border.

MAKING THE MOST OF COLOUR

In many respects it is the overall form or outline of plants, together with the shape and texture of their foliage, that is the real worth of a well-planned border. Flowers are almost a bonus and, in many cases, on show for only a limited time. It is nevertheless important to understand how colour works in the garden.

The hot colours – red, orange and yellow – are always dominant, drawing the eye. If these are placed at the bottom of a garden or view they will demand your attention and tend to foreshorten the space. Pastels, on the other hand, are far less demanding. In principle, if you group the hot colours close to the house or main viewpoint and the pastel colours further away, this will enhance the feeling of space as the eye is drawn more slowly down the garden. Grey, present in the foliage of many plants, is a great harmonizer, softening the hot colours and drawing colour ranges together.

53

▽ **THE BEAUTY OF** *a herbaceous border lies in the tiered effect of plants at different heights, furnishing colour and interest all summer. The pergola is clothed with climbing roses, Rosa 'New Dawn' and* Rosa multiflora, *while tall delphiniums provide impact in the middle of the border.*

SUITING THE SOIL

Remember that certain types of plant enjoy quite different kinds of soil. There is little point growing ericaceous plants, such as azaleas, rhododendron and pieris (*see picture below*) or summer-flowering heathers in alkaline or chalky soil as they will never be happy. Some plants prefer moist soil and others like dry conditions, so always check the soil type and conditions into which you will be planting. Bear in mind too that any soil benefits from the addition of organic material such as well-rotted compost and manure, so add this at the time of planting to ensure your plants have a good start.

A border for year-round interest

Everybody's ideal border is one that looks good for 365 days of the year and this is a true test of the skill of your planting. Although it is difficult to make a border as colourful in winter as it is in high summer, with careful planning there is no reason why a winter border should lack interest. The secret is a balance of evergreen and deciduous plants, carefully selected for different flowering times, strong shapes and leaf texture.

54

THE BORDER IN SUMMER

When you plan for summer, think of the richness of the planting palette and the overall character of individual plants rather than going for brash flower colours. Put together plants whose habit or leaf texture complement each other and regard their flowers as a bonus. This border relies at one end on the contrasting leaves of acanthus and *Vitis coignetiae,* with the stunning blue flowers of ceanothus and *Hebe* 'Midsummer Beauty' providing extra impact. Towards the other end, the netted gold leaves of the honeysuckle offset the delicate, upright grass, *Miscanthus sinensis* 'Nippon'.

▷ **WINTER IS THE SEASON** *when the shape of plants and evergreen foliage come into their own. At the back of this border the honeysuckle retains most of its leaves, softening the fence. Spiky yuccas look good at any time of year, while escallonia, broom,* Euphorbia polychroma *and* Stachys byzantina *are all evergreen.*

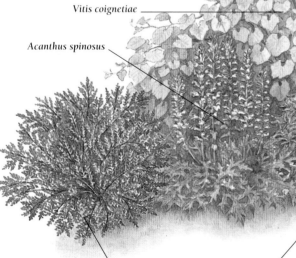

Delphinium

Hibiscus syriacus 'Woodbridge'

Crambe cordifolia

Vitis coignetiae

Acanthus spinosus

Spiraea japonica 'Goldflame'

Hebe 'Midsummer Beauty'

Ceanothus burkwoodii

Potentilla fruticosa 'Tangerine'

Yucca filamentosa

Euphorbia polychroma

▷ **SPRING BORDERS** *set the theme for the coming season. The golden-leaved robinia tree contrasts with the glossy green foliage of the flowered choisya on one side and the lavatera on the other. Groups of red- and cream-flowered tulips behind the geraniums provide colourful spring highlights.*

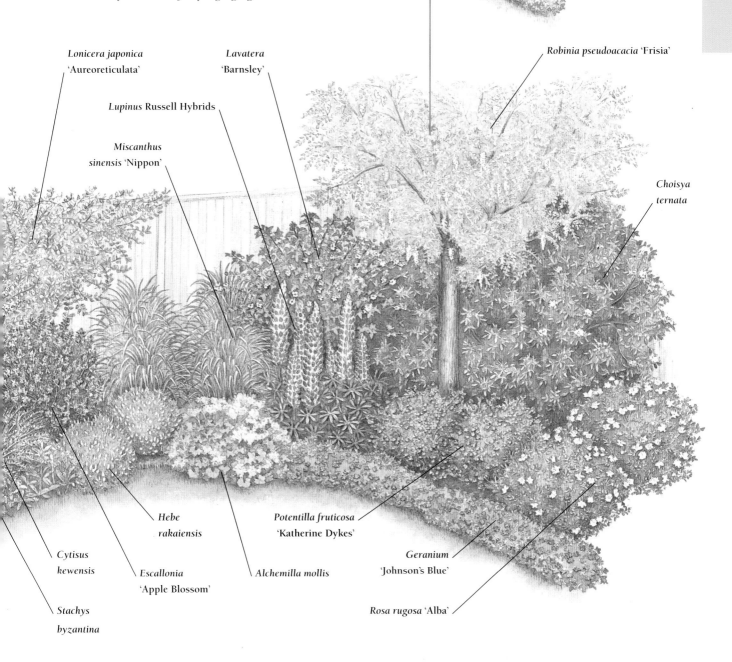

Lonicera japonica 'Aureoreticulata'

Lavatera 'Barnsley'

Robinia pseudoacacia 'Frisia'

Lupinus Russell Hybrids

Miscanthus sinensis 'Nippon'

Choisya ternata

Hebe rakaiensis

Potentilla fruticosa 'Katherine Dykes'

Cytisus kewensis

Escallonia 'Apple Blossom'

Alchemilla mollis

Geranium 'Johnson's Blue'

Stachys byzantina

Rosa rugosa 'Alba'

Creating a theme

While the divisions and hard landscape of a garden provide its structure and its framework, it will be plants that animate it and the overall feel of your garden will be determined by the species you choose. As there is a variety of different environments in most gardens, it makes sense to select plants whose cultural needs suit their situation as well as keeping to a clear design theme.

56

PLANTING FOR A SHADY WALL

Many people despair of the shady areas in their garden, but there are many species that will thrive in such a situation. This shady wall is almost completely obscured by evergreens: the rhododendron, with its handsome flowers and foliage, is flanked by hypericum and winter jasmine, both yellow-flowered although blooming at different times of year, and *Viburnum tinus* has deliciously fragrant flowers in winter. Spring-flowering hellebores and bergenias sprawl closer to ground level.

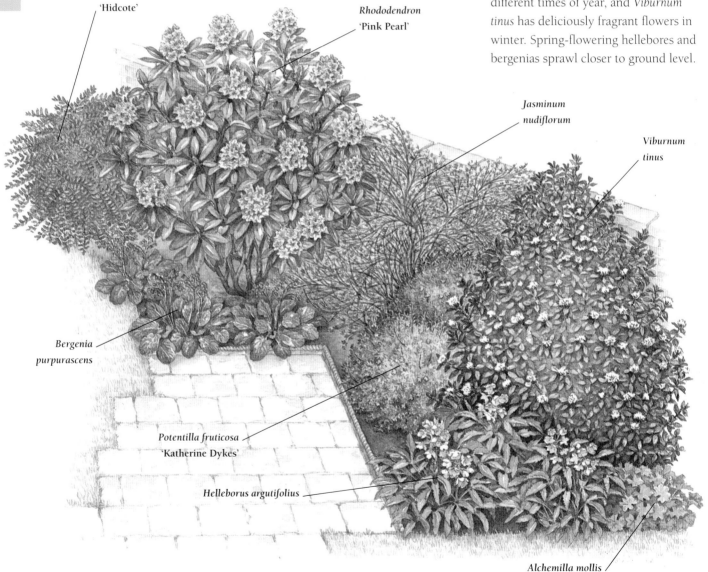

Hypericum 'Hidcote'

Rhododendron 'Pink Pearl'

Jasminum nudiflorum

Viburnum tinus

Bergenia purpurascens

Potentilla fruticosa 'Katherine Dykes'

Helleborus argutifolius

Alchemilla mollis

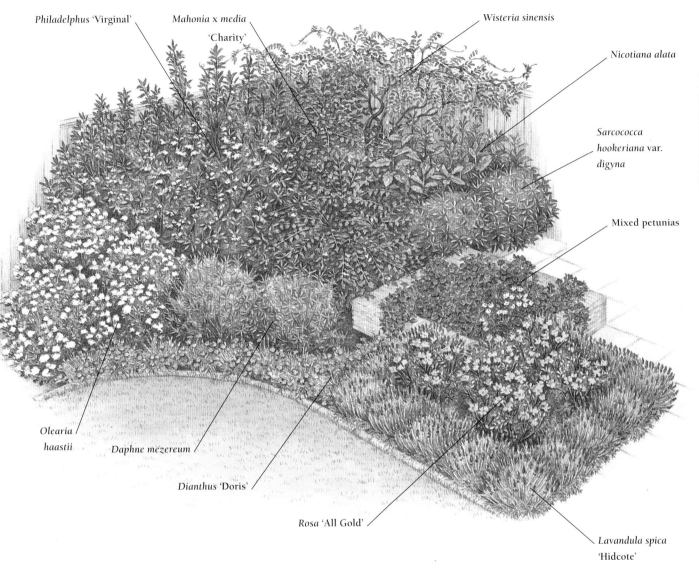

Philadelphus 'Virginal'

Mahonia x media 'Charity'

Wisteria sinensis

Nicotiana alata

Sarcococca hookeriana var. *digyna*

Mixed petunias

Olearia haastii

Daphne mezereum

Dianthus 'Doris'

Rosa 'All Gold'

Lavandula spica 'Hidcote'

A FRAGRANT BORDER

I try always to plan fragrant areas into my gardens, choosing places that will most benefit from scented flower and foliage. A bed like this would be ideal close to French doors opening on to a generous terrace or flanking a summer house in a more distant part of the garden. The scent of lavender is released as you brush past it, while philadelphus (mock orange) is one of the most strongly perfumed of all garden plants. Evenings would bring the fragrance of wisteria and night-scented tobacco plants. Daphne, sarcococca and the daisy bush (*Olearia haastii*) all exude more unusual scents.

Three treatments

There are unlimited ways in which to design a garden but to be successful any plot should reflect the owner's personality and lifestyle, which is why it is never a good idea to simply copy a garden from a book, a television programme or a flower show. Use such gardens as inspiration by all means, but always try to give your design a personal hallmark. The three designs for the same plot shown here reflect individual approaches.

58

SIMPLE CURVES

In this simple, naturalistic layout, the design is built up from a series of strong, flowing curves. The surface is mainly lawn, with a path sweeping up to the top of the garden where it terminates at the seat, which also acts as a focal point. A successful device is the wing of planting that divides up the space so that not everything is visible at a single glance. The creation of a feeling of mystery and surprise is effective even in a small space.

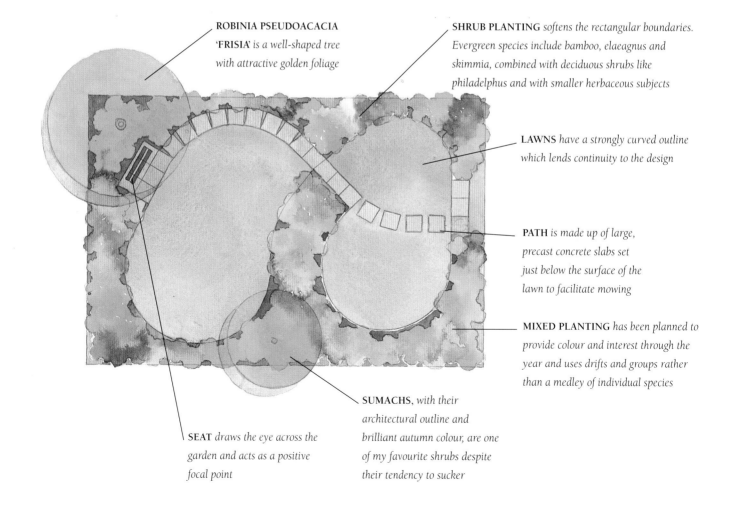

ROBINIA PSEUDOACACIA *'FRISIA' is a well-shaped tree with attractive golden foliage*

SHRUB PLANTING *softens the rectangular boundaries. Evergreen species include bamboo, elaeagnus and skimmia, combined with deciduous shrubs like philadelphus and with smaller herbaceous subjects*

LAWNS *have a strongly curved outline which lends continuity to the design*

PATH *is made up of large, precast concrete slabs set just below the surface of the lawn to facilitate mowing*

MIXED PLANTING *has been planned to provide colour and interest through the year and uses drifts and groups rather than a medley of individual species*

SUMACHS, *with their architectural outline and brilliant autumn colour, are one of my favourite shrubs despite their tendency to sucker*

SEAT *draws the eye across the garden and acts as a positive focal point*

THE ESSENTIAL GARDEN

This slightly more structured design, with a central lawn, again uses curves to suggest movement but allows more room for sitting and dining as well as space for a utility area, or shed, in the far corner. This is a fairly basic garden design that is flexible enough to have other features 'bolted on' to it at a later date.

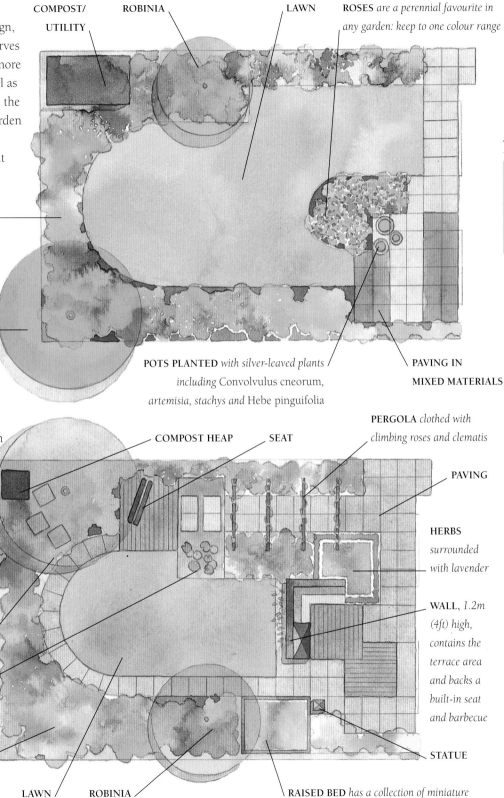

**COMPOST/
UTILITY**

ROBINIA

LAWN

ROSES *are a perennial favourite in any garden: keep to one colour range*

MIXED PLANTING *screens next door's garage, using* Viburnum tinus, *holly, miscanthus and* Elaeagnus ebbingii *'Limelight'*

APPLE TREE

POTS PLANTED *with silver-leaved plants including* Convolvulus cneorum, *artemisia, stachys and* Hebe pinguifolia

**PAVING IN
MIXED MATERIALS**

DEVELOPING THE THEME

This more sophisticated design is a logical progression of the garden above, introducing a path that sweeps away from the extended terrace to pause at the seat placed on the brick paving. Stepping stones cross the pool and return to the house, passing under the pergola flanked by planting.

COMPOST HEAP

SEAT

PERGOLA *clothed with climbing roses and clematis*

PAVING

HERBS *surrounded with lavender*

WALL, *1.2m (4ft) high, contains the terrace area and backs a built-in seat and barbecue*

APPLE TREE

A POOL *is a delightful element in any garden. Stepping stones are set just above the water's surface*

MIXED PLANTING *clothes the boundaries: there are plants for interest in all seasons*

LAWN

ROBINIA

STATUE

RAISED BED *has a collection of miniature conifers that look effective grouped together*

Low-maintenance garden

Maintenance, or lack of it, is often in the eye of the owner. There is a fine distinction between just pottering and more serious work in a garden and the key to minimizing the upkeep required is a sensible balance between hard and soft landscape.

A good combination of shrubs, herbaceous perennials and ground cover will knit together to keep maintenance to a minimum once the planting is established.

HIGH INTEREST, LOW UPKEEP

This garden, for a hard-working couple with limited leisure time, was designed to look interesting but need minimum maintenance. The rectangular site, typical of the plots behind thousands of newly built homes, measures 10m by 7m (33ft by 23ft) and slopes gently up, away from the house. As the garden is small, the whole design has been turned on the diagonal to help create a feeling of greater space.

The generous terrace is paved in simulated natural stone flags with inserts of brick to give a visual link with the house. A small, raised pool adds interest and steps climb up to the strongly curved lawn, its outline emphasized by a brick edging, that provides visual movement in the centre of the garden. Planting, consisting of low-maintenance shrubs with flowering bulbs and perennials, wraps all around the lawn.

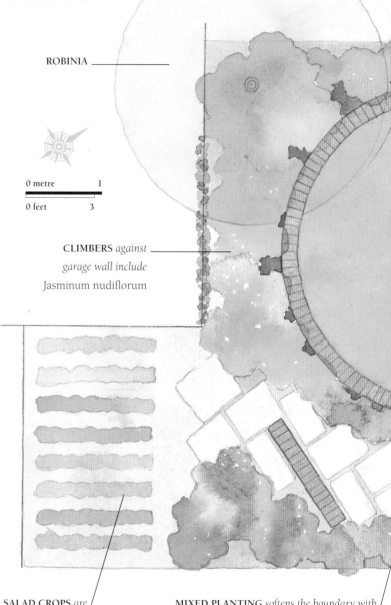

ROBINIA

0 metre   1
0 feet   3

CLIMBERS *against garage wall include* Jasminum nudiflorum

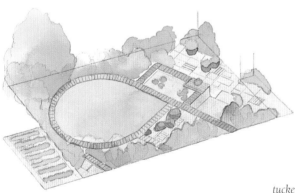

SALAD CROPS *are tucked away in an awkward corner of the garden*

MIXED PLANTING *softens the boundary with* potentilla, Spiraea japonica *'Goldflame'*, Alchemilla mollis; Clematis montana *clothes the fence*

PLANTING *includes a mix of shrubs and herbaceous perennials, with sweeps of Geranium endressii and G. x riversleaianum 'Russell Prichard' at the front of the border*

FORMAL POOL *is raised 45cm (18in) above terrace level and fitted with a simple bubble fountain. One corner is formed into a plinth for a large pot*

CLIMBERS INCLUDE *Clematis tangutica and Vitis vinifera 'Purpurea'*

BRICK EDGING *makes mowing easier*

POTS PLANTED *with a collection of alpines such as arabis, saxifrages, sedum and gentians*

IMITATION STONE SLABS *are interspersed with random brick paving*

STEPS UP

PLANTING *by the house consists of a fragrant sarcococca, underplanted with ground-covering periwinkle*

IN THIS SHADY *part of the garden, planting includes euonymus, hostas and bergenias, with Hydrangea petiolaris on the fence*

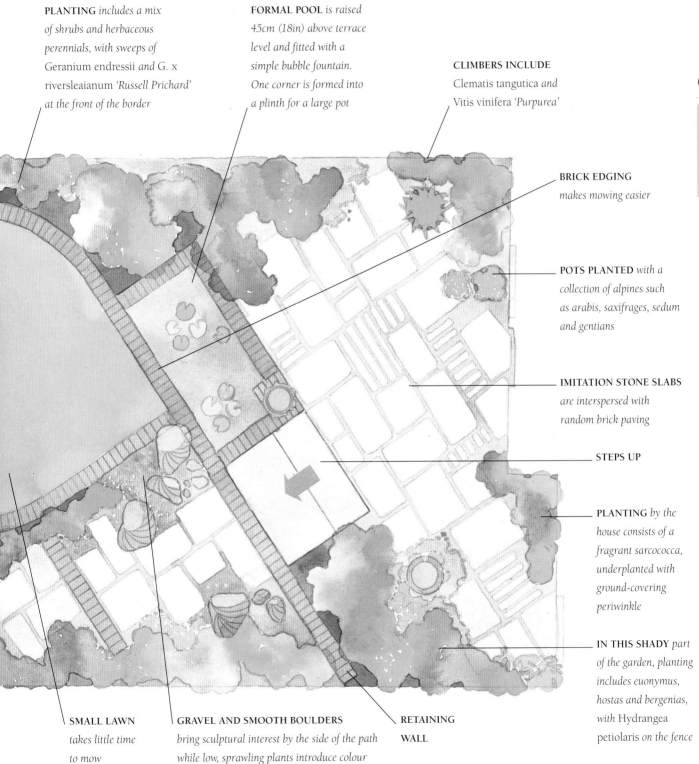

SMALL LAWN *takes little time to mow*

GRAVEL AND SMOOTH BOULDERS *bring sculptural interest by the side of the path while low, sprawling plants introduce colour*

RETAINING WALL

Family garden

Children, grandchildren or just friends' children will all appreciate a garden that really works for them. This will usually involve the provision of enough hard surfacing close to the house, a lawn that is hard-wearing enough for boisterous play and, if possible, a path running right around the garden for wheeled toys and vehicles. If you can add to this colourful flowers and foliage and a bed set aside for child-orientated planting, you may well have budding young gardeners on your hands.

62

CATERING FOR ALL NEEDS

This amply sized family garden was designed to provide for a wide range of different activities. Moving away from the house, the terrace is generous enough for play as well as for relaxation and outdoor meals. The raised sandpit has a removable cover and could be replaced later by a raised bed for planting or by a raised pool. A path sweeps away around the garden, leading the eye away from the rectangular boundaries and giving access to the salad crops and the slide, set in rougher grass. Planting softens the whole area and a predominance of tough species will still look good, notwithstanding the ravages of the odd football or errant tricycle.

The main play areas and equipment are in view from the house windows, an important safety aspect. Planting in front of the windows has been kept low, using small shrubs, so it does not obscure the view.

SLIDE

SHED

APPLE TREE *set in longer grass, naturalized with bulbs*

SALAD CROPS *take up less space than a vegetable plot but ensure fresh produce. Many salads are also ideal crops for children to grow, giving quick returns*

COMPOST HEAP *screened by beech hedge*

BEECH HEDGE

SORBUS ARIA 'LUTESCENS' *is an excellent small garden tree whose silvery-grey leaves look wonderful in spring*

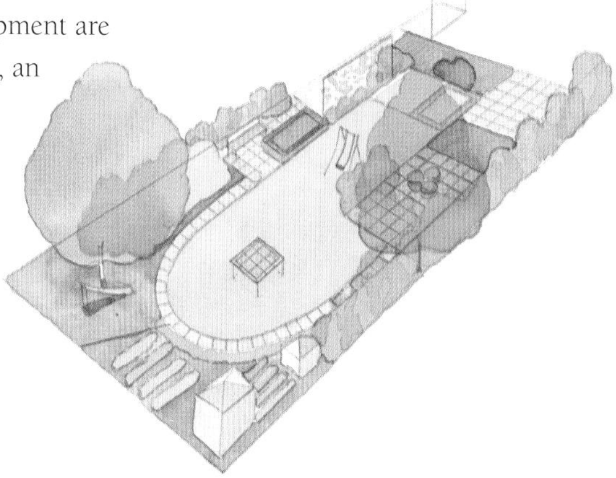

MIXED BORDER *contains some big plants – fragrant buddleja for butterflies, lavatera for wonderful flowers and plenty of huge, cheerful sunflowers, loved by children. Added to this are sedums, also for butterflies, and instant annuals, sown in drifts through the border*

CLIMBING FRAME

SEAT

SWING *within view of house*

HERBS SURROUNDED *by lavender provide a fragrant feature conveniently close to the kitchen. Let children trim off the lavender spikes, once flowering is over, to make lavender bags*

SPACE FOR *rotary clothes drier*

SCREEN *made from simple, squared trellis hosts brightly flowered runner beans mixed with white sweet peas*

0 metre 3
0 feet 10

BRICK PAVING

SUN-LOVING *colourful plants include small shrubs like cistus, hebe, senecio, phlomis and cytisus, with herbaceous species of hosta, geum and dianthus*

RAISED SANDPIT

BRICK PAVING

TOUGH SHRUBS *include potentilla, spiraea, garrya, weigela, viburnum and hydrangea, with wisteria on the fence*

POTS PLANTED *with bright annuals such as nasturtiums and petunias: children can sow the seeds and watch them develop*

Two front gardens

First impressions count, which is why the front garden is an important space that should look good throughout the year. There is no excuse for a front garden to look drab and neglected, as is all too often the case. In constant use, front gardens often have to cater for car parking as well as access by people. Since this space is usually of limited dimensions whether or not it includes car parking, simplicity is generally the key to a successful design.

64

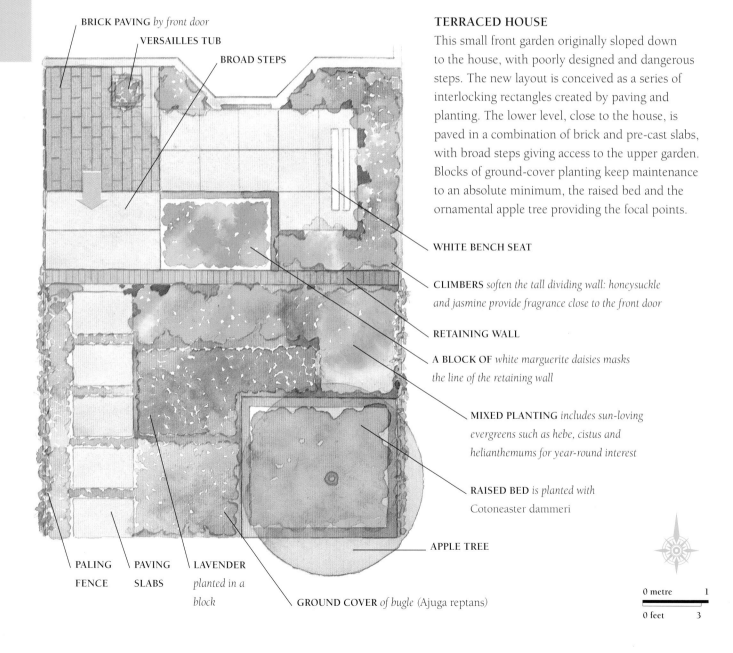

BRICK PAVING *by front door*

VERSAILLES TUB

BROAD STEPS

PALING FENCE

PAVING SLABS

LAVENDER *planted in a block*

GROUND COVER *of bugle (Ajuga reptans)*

TERRACED HOUSE

This small front garden originally sloped down to the house, with poorly designed and dangerous steps. The new layout is conceived as a series of interlocking rectangles created by paving and planting. The lower level, close to the house, is paved in a combination of brick and pre-cast slabs, with broad steps giving access to the upper garden. Blocks of ground-cover planting keep maintenance to an absolute minimum, the raised bed and the ornamental apple tree providing the focal points.

WHITE BENCH SEAT

CLIMBERS *soften the tall dividing wall: honeysuckle and jasmine provide fragrance close to the front door*

RETAINING WALL

A BLOCK OF *white marguerite daisies masks the line of the retaining wall*

MIXED PLANTING *includes sun-loving evergreens such as hebe, cistus and helianthemums for year-round interest*

RAISED BED *is planted with* Cotoneaster dammeri

APPLE TREE

0 metre 1

0 feet 3

FRONT GARDEN WITH DRIVE

As this front garden incorporates a driveway for cars, minimal maintenance was
called for, so either side of the drive is surfaced with gravel and smooth boulders,
laid over a permeable 'weed mat'. Paving gives access to both the front and side
of the house, with plants in pots and the raised bed supplying colour and
interest. Planting elsewhere softens the garden, the purple-leaved birches casting
dappled shade and providing a vertical emphasis.

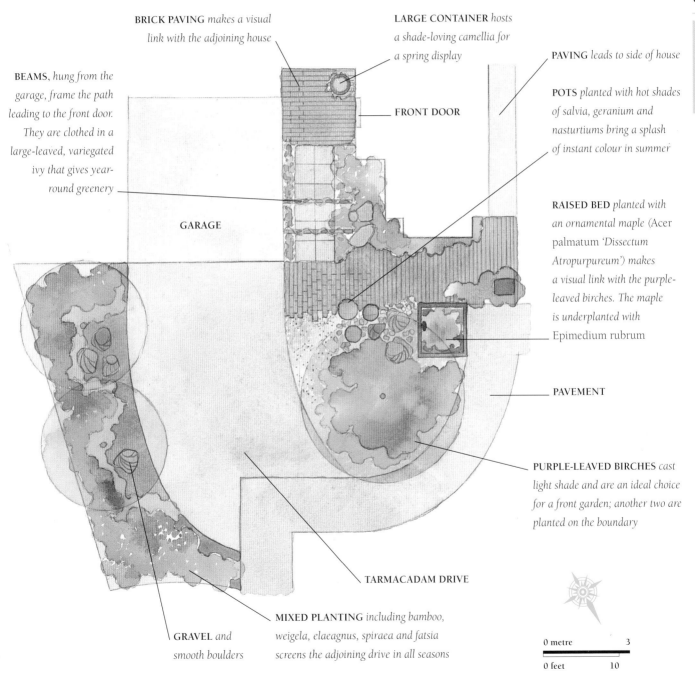

BRICK PAVING *makes a visual
link with the adjoining house*

LARGE CONTAINER *hosts
a shade-loving camellia for
a spring display*

PAVING *leads to side of house*

POTS *planted with hot shades
of salvia, geranium and
nasturtiums bring a splash
of instant colour in summer*

BEAMS, *hung from the
garage, frame the path
leading to the front door.
They are clothed in a
large-leaved, variegated
ivy that gives year-
round greenery*

FRONT DOOR

RAISED BED *planted with
an ornamental maple (Acer
palmatum 'Dissectum
Atropurpureum') makes
a visual link with the purple-
leaved birches. The maple
is underplanted with
Epimedium rubrum*

GARAGE

PAVEMENT

PURPLE-LEAVED BIRCHES *cast
light shade and are an ideal choice
for a front garden; another two are
planted on the boundary*

TARMACADAM DRIVE

GRAVEL *and
smooth boulders*

MIXED PLANTING *including bamboo,
weigela, elaeagnus, spiraea and fatsia
screens the adjoining drive in all seasons*

0 metre   3

0 feet   10

Roof terrace

Roof gardens, terraces and balconies make delightful gardens, often with spectacular views, but they have their own particular difficulties, chiefly concerned with load-bearing, high winds and problems of access. Since this is the only outdoor space available to many city dwellers, it is worth undertaking any structural work required to make the garden safe; the reward will be a verdant oasis perched high above the streets.

66

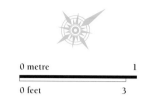

0 metre   1
0 feet   3

A GARDEN IN THE SKY

This tiny roof garden measures just 5m by 5m (16ft by 16ft) and nestles between two sides of the building and a dividing wall that separates it from the house next door. The fourth side is open, looking across a skyscape of roof tiles and chimneys.

As this was a relatively new building, the sub-structure of the roof had been designed to support a living space as well as to provide access, but anyone contemplating this kind of project should *always check the roof's load-bearing capacity with an architect or structural engineer before proceeding.* As the strongest part of most roofs is around the edges, this is where the main weight is distributed, in this case in the form of raised beds and a small pool. The raised beds are built from lightweight blocks that were rendered and painted a warm, earthy colour. They are filled with lightweight compost and watered by automatic irrigation. The pool is fitted with a butyl liner.

The floor is paved in a combination of lightweight, square tiles and thin terracotta tiles, the latter forming a grid that ties the composition together visually. Decking would be another lightweight alternative. The front of the garden has a glass screen to provide shelter while making the most of the view.

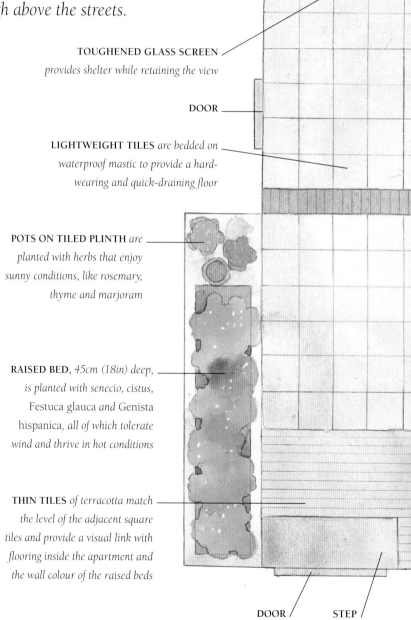

TOUGHENED GLASS SCREEN *provides shelter while retaining the view*

DOOR

LIGHTWEIGHT TILES *are bedded on waterproof mastic to provide a hard-wearing and quick-draining floor*

POTS ON TILED PLINTH *are planted with herbs that enjoy sunny conditions, like rosemary, thyme and marjoram*

RAISED BED, *45cm (18in) deep, is planted with senecio, cistus, Festuca glauca and Genista hispanica, all of which tolerate wind and thrive in hot conditions*

THIN TILES *of terracotta match the level of the adjacent square tiles and provide a visual link with flooring inside the apartment and the wall colour of the raised beds*

DOOR /   **STEP** /

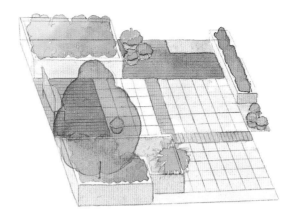

RAISED POOL *is built from lightweight blocks and lined with a butyl sheet; aquatic plants and fish thrive here. A small submersible pump provides a bubble fountain*

APPLE TREE *grown on a dwarfing rootstock is ideal in a limited space; it is planted in the raised bed and secured to the adjoining wall*

LARGE RAISED BED *contains sun-loving shrubs such as helianthemum,* phlomis, Convolvulus cneorum *and* Hebe pinguifolia 'Pagei'

LARGE CONTAINER *planted with yellow marguerite daisies in summer*

SEAT *placed to enjoy the pool*

HIGH BOUNDARY WALL

RAISED BED *contains* Ceanothus thyrsiflorus *var.* repens, Salvia officinalis, Cytisus battandieri *and* yucca. *All these plants will need regular feeding*

TERRACOTTA POTS *host a collection of colourful bulbs in spring and annual bedding in summer*

Dog-leg garden

Gardens that run around two sides of a house, or where one part of the plot is not visible from the house, are quite common and the challenge in design terms is to provide continuity. All too often this results in a missed opportunity because only one section of the garden is developed or drawn together into an overall composition. The appeal of a 'dog-leg' shaped plot is the feeling of mystery and surprise as you are encouraged from one area of the garden into another, where a whole range of features and opportunities opens up.

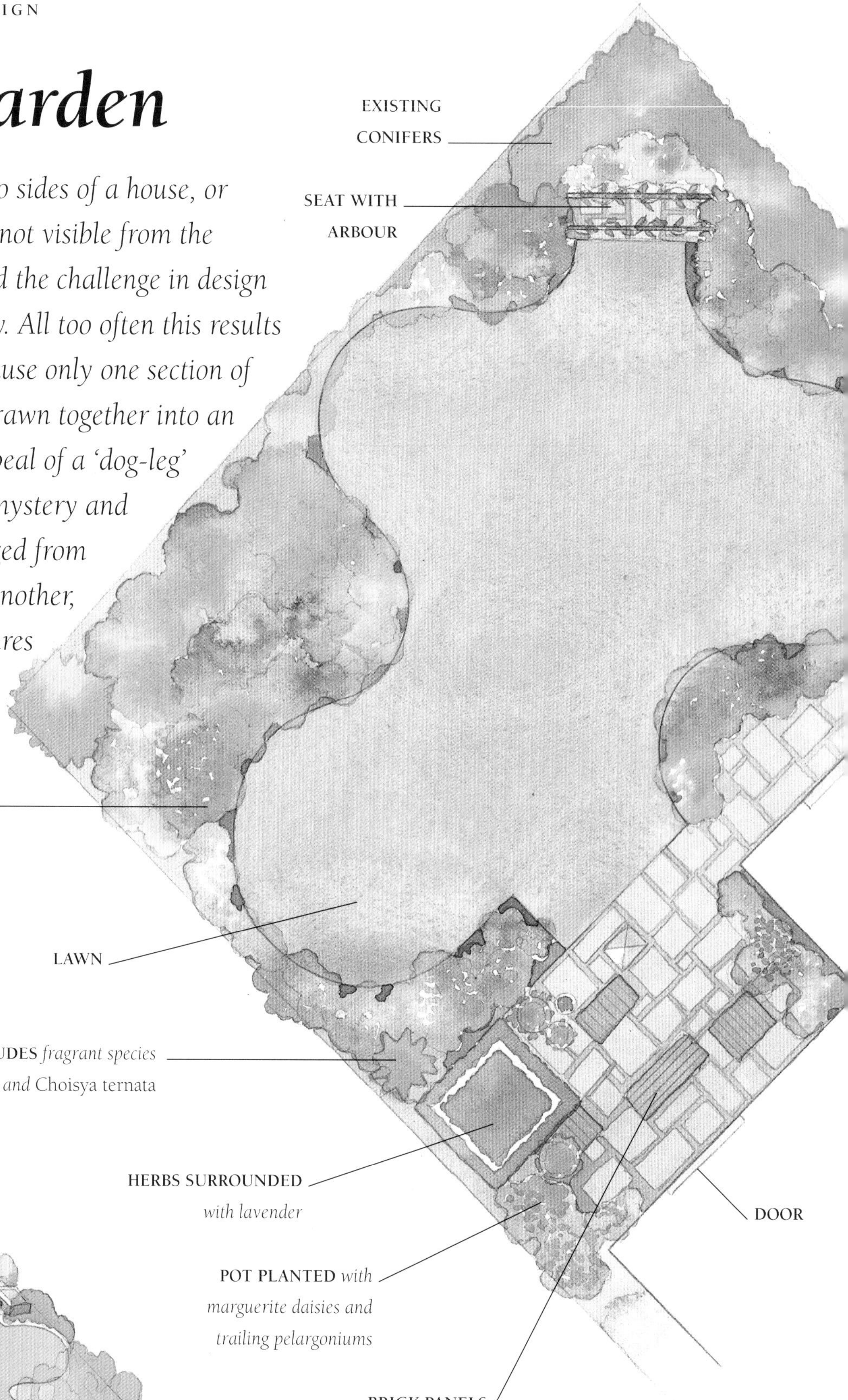

68

EXISTING
CONIFERS

SEAT WITH
ARBOUR

MIXED PLANTING
softens the hard fence line with a combination of shrubs and herbaceous perennials, including weigela, spiraea, potentilla, lupins, geum and euphorbias

LAWN

PLANTING INCLUDES fragrant species such as roses, lilies and Choisya ternata

HERBS SURROUNDED
with lavender

POT PLANTED with marguerite daisies and trailing pelargoniums

BRICK PANELS
set between natural stone slabs

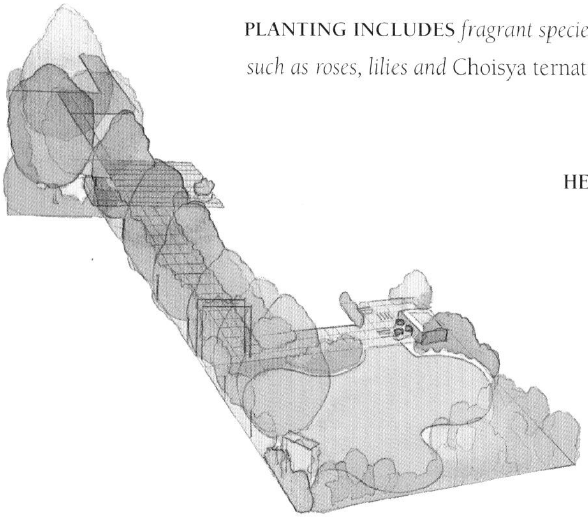

DOOR

SUNNY BORDER *uses sweeps of ground-covering shrubs and herbaceous perennials, including* Geranium *'Johnson's Blue',* Stachys byzantina *and* Hebe pinguifolia *'Pagei' to keep maintenance low*

A TOUR ROUND THE GARDEN
In this plot, the 'side' garden is a narrow passage that opens out from a conservatory attached to the house and in full view from it. Pine trees filled the space and, once these were thinned, a delightful walkway of stepping stones through ground cover was created to lead naturally to the more open garden at the rear of the house. When you turn the corner, a clematis-covered arch provides a sense of expectation as the

view through to the main garden opens out. Once in the larger garden area, with access from both the dining and sitting rooms of the house, there is a real feeling of space and movement, with a flowing area of lawn and well-stocked flower borders. There is ample room for sitting and dining on the terrace, which is paved with a mixture of brick and natural stone slabs. Herbs provide fragrance and easy pickings close to the kitchen.

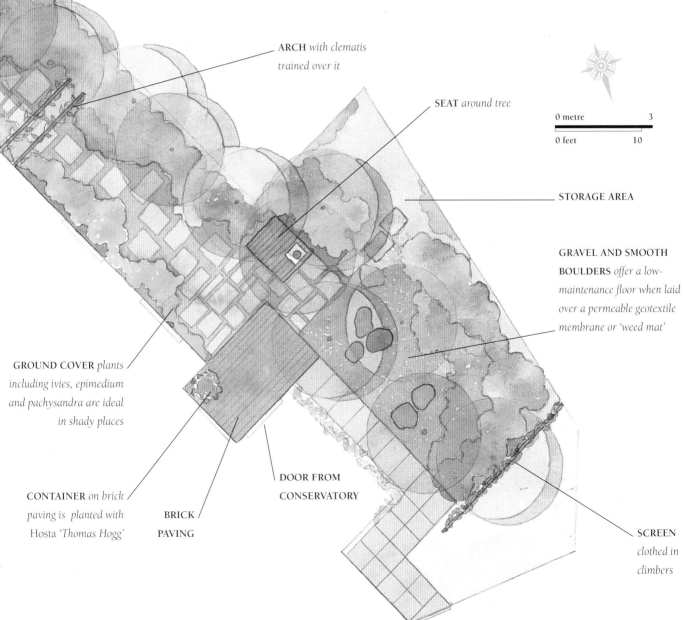

ARCH *with clematis trained over it*

SEAT *around tree*

0 metre   3
0 feet   10

STORAGE AREA

GRAVEL AND SMOOTH BOULDERS *offer a low-maintenance floor when laid over a permeable geotextile membrane or 'weed mat'*

GROUND COVER *plants including ivies, epimedium and pachysandra are ideal in shady places*

CONTAINER *on brick paving is planted with* Hosta *'Thomas Hogg'*

BRICK PAVING

DOOR FROM CONSERVATORY

SCREEN *clothed in climbers*

Long, narrow garden

Town gardens are often long and thin, particularly those outside older properties that interlock with one another to produce awkwardly aligned boundaries. Such gardens can frequently be shady and overlooked but they form perfect outdoor rooms with plenty of shelter. Given a design that aims to break up the length visually, and with carefully chosen hard surfacing, architectural plants and minimal maintenance, small can often mean beautiful.

70

TINY TOWN PLOT

This restricted site is barely 13m long by 6m wide (43ft by 20ft) in the main part of the garden. Access is from the kitchen door on to a lower terrace, floored in old York stone and courses of brick that aim to widen the space visually. A change of level is used as a means of dividing up the space and adding interest. A single, broad step leads to the upper garden level, where you pass beneath an arch and up to a compact little painted shed. Planting along the boundaries is vitally important to soften the line of the surrounding walls and prevent the garden from being overlooked or feeling too closed in.

FONT, *found at an antique sale, makes a wonderful plant container*

ARCH *provides spatial division between the two garden levels and leads to the shed*

SMALL TREE

POTS

SPACE *for rotary clothes drier*

POT PLANTED *with large-leaved hosta*

MIXED PLANTING *on this sunny side of the garden includes ceanothus, senecio, hibiscus, datura and summer-flowering jasmine*

SMALL SHED *is brightly painted*

COMPOST HEAP OR STORAGE

0 metre   1

0 feet   3

MULTI-STEMMED BIRCH *as a screen*

MIXED PLANTING *includes ferns and hostas*

POTS PLANTED *with annuals*

MIXED PLANTING *includes hellebores, astilbes, hemerocallis and* Euphorbia wulfenii

CLEMATIS *'Nelly Moser'*

SEAT

POT PLANTED *with camellia*

POT PLANTED *with variegated ivies*

DOOR

CLEMATIS

BRICK *courses laid within the York stone helps to relieve the overall expanse*

GATE

PAVING *of random old York stone slabs*

CLEMATIS TANGUTICA *looks wonderful on a shady wall, with its bell-shaped yellow flowers and feathery seedheads that last into winter*

POTS FILLED *with ericaceous compost and planted with pieris, camellia and Japanese azalea*

RAISED BED *holds a collection of hellebores and hostas, beneath* Garrya elliptica

RETAINING WALL *and top step*

POTS WITH *a collection of ferns*

SHADE PLANTING *includes aucuba, bamboos, skimmia, sarcococca,* Viburnum davidii *and* Fatsia japonica. *All are evergreen and provide year-round interest*

A sloping site

Sloping gardens can provide far greater interest than a flat site but they may also cost a good deal more to construct. Creating a series of changes of level involves the building of retaining walls, steps, ramps and terracing in order to provide several flat, usable areas. Always bear in mind that a garden which slopes up, in front of you, tends visually to foreshorten the space, while one that drops away from you has the opposite effect.

72

CHANGES IN LEVEL

The slope in this garden is just under 2m (6ft) from the top end of the garden to the bottom and the space has been organized into a flat terrace close to the house and a level lawn in the middle. Steps climb the bank to the left, terminating by an arbour at the highest point of the garden; the seat enclosed within the arbour looks out over the pool, with its rocky outcrops and tumbling waterfall. Planting softens and surrounds the garden, detracting the eye from those awkward boundaries.

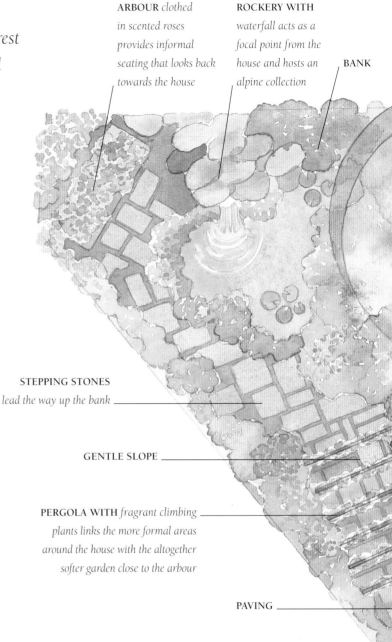

ARBOUR *clothed in scented roses provides informal seating that looks back towards the house*

ROCKERY WITH *waterfall acts as a focal point from the house and hosts an alpine collection*

BANK

STEPPING STONES *lead the way up the bank*

GENTLE SLOPE

PERGOLA WITH *fragrant climbing plants links the more formal areas around the house with the altogether softer garden close to the arbour*

PAVING

MIXED PLANTING *throughout the garden is a combination of shrubs and herbaceous perennials, with evergreens for winter interest*

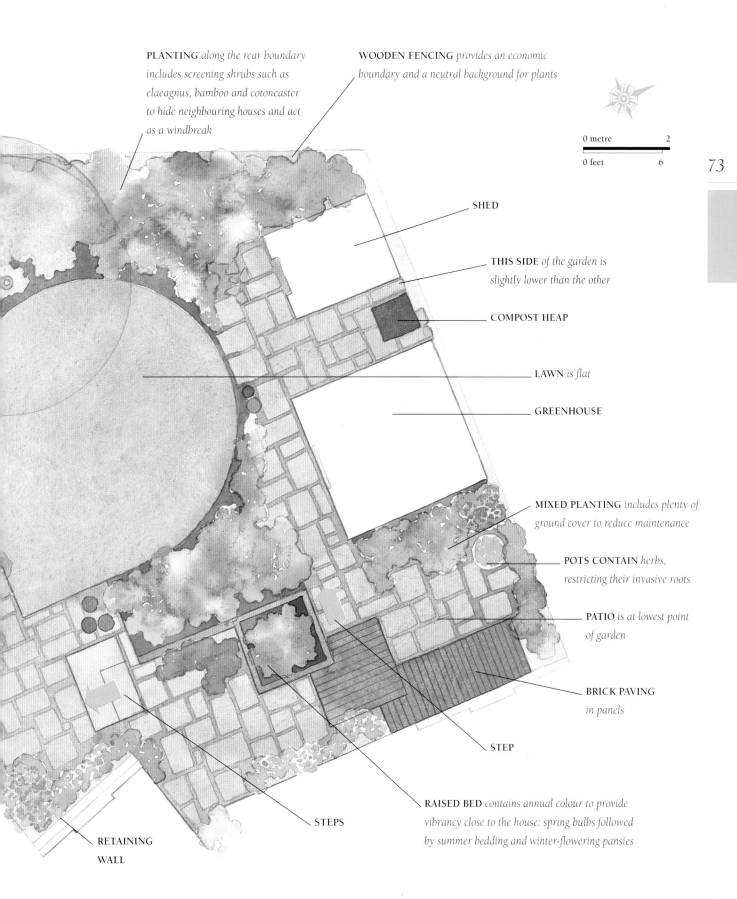

PLANTING *along the rear boundary includes screening shrubs such as elaeagnus, bamboo and cotoneaster to hide neighbouring houses and act as a windbreak*

WOODEN FENCING *provides an economic boundary and a neutral background for plants*

0 metre 2
0 feet 6

SHED

THIS SIDE *of the garden is slightly lower than the other*

COMPOST HEAP

LAWN *is flat*

GREENHOUSE

MIXED PLANTING *includes plenty of ground cover to reduce maintenance*

POTS CONTAIN *herbs, restricting their invasive roots*

PATIO *is at lowest point of garden*

BRICK PAVING *in panels*

STEP

RAISED BED *contains annual colour to provide vibrancy close to the house: spring bulbs followed by summer bedding and winter-flowering pansies*

STEPS

RETAINING WALL

A formal garden

Formal gardens have a naturally static, traditional feel and offer a controlled sense of space based on symmetry. They have a balance from one side of the design to the other and rely on a single axis or a number of well-defined axes to divide the area up into a pattern of compartments or rooms that can be given over to different individual themes. Formal designs tend to look best adjoining a period or modern house that has a regular, classical, often somewhat plain facade that is formal in character.

74

MIRROR IMAGE

This garden adjoins a small modern town house with a single French window giving access to a slightly raised terrace. The terrace is paved in a combination of bricks and pre-cast concrete slabs, the brick paving in the middle providing a visual link with the building. Broad steps lead down to the central lawn, flanked by two inward-facing seats.

The rectangular plot is divided lengthways into two halves, with two 'wings' of wall or trellis separating the first from the second. The central path that forms the main axis passes beneath a pergola and ends at the summer house situated at the far end of the garden. Two smaller lawns and identical trees strengthen the sense of formality, at the same time providing balance and visual stability.

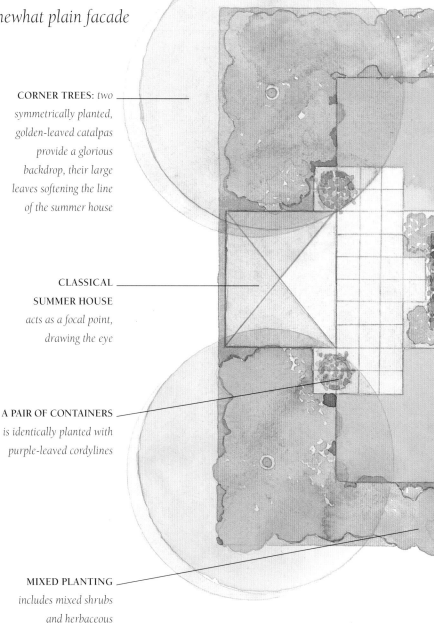

CORNER TREES: *two symmetrically planted, golden-leaved catalpas provide a glorious backdrop, their large leaves softening the line of the summer house*

CLASSICAL SUMMER HOUSE *acts as a focal point, drawing the eye*

A PAIR OF CONTAINERS *is identically planted with purple-leaved cordylines*

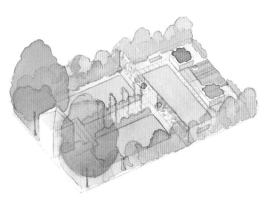

MIXED PLANTING *includes mixed shrubs and herbaceous perennials in cool colours*

0 metre   2

0 feet   6

THE PERGOLA *reinforces the central axis, leading down to the summer house. It is clad with climbing roses in pale colours*

MIXED PLANTING *here is designed in hotter colours that work well close to the main terrace and viewpoint*

SEATS *in Lutyens design*

LAWN

LAWN

RAISED BED

PAVING *of sand-coloured concrete slabs*

CLIMBERS *on house wall include fragrant summer jasmine and roses*

LARGE TERRACOTTA POTS *are simply planted with white marguerite daisies*

BRICK PAVING *matches bricks in the house*

CLIMBERS

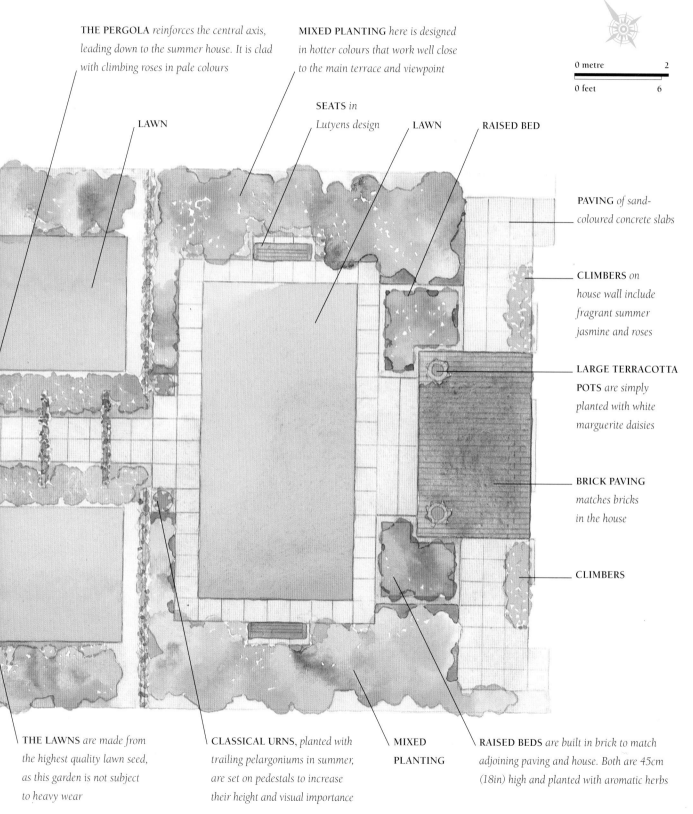

THE LAWNS *are made from the highest quality lawn seed, as this garden is not subject to heavy wear*

CLASSICAL URNS, *planted with trailing pelargoniums in summer, are set on pedestals to increase their height and visual importance*

MIXED PLANTING

RAISED BEDS *are built in brick to match adjoining paving and house. Both are 45cm (18in) high and planted with aromatic herbs*

Wrap-around garden

In many situations, a detached house may stand right in the middle of its plot, with the garden forming an envelope of spaces that flow from one to another. A successful design will not only reinforce this feeling of continuity but at the same time also allow each area to have its own identity or specific purpose. This can present a challenge, especially if the dimensions of each section of garden are limited, but it should still be possible to harness the sense of flowing space.

76

SMALL SIDE LAWN
has a strong shape

LARGE CONTAINER
*gives a focus in entrance
to first garden area*

MIXED PLANTING
includes shade-loving plants

A FLUID DESIGN

The beauty of this garden unfolds as you move around the house. The simple semi-circle of the side lawn is screened from the main garden by a trellis and arch. Once you have passed through this, the strongly formed composition provides real movement as the curved path sweeps beneath the pergola and leads round to the seat and arbour in the far corner of the main garden. The sitting area with water is paved with random, rectangular slabs, the water feature bringing sound, movement and interest. Moving on again, the overhead beams give way to a formal herb bed and vegetable garden. So while each area has its own character and purpose, the design links them seamlessly together.

GREENHOUSE

CLIMBERS *are trained against fence*

COMPOST HEAP

A VEGETABLE PLOT *fills the awkward shape between house and boundary. Greenhouse, compost heap and shed all have a practical function; runner beans are trained against fence*

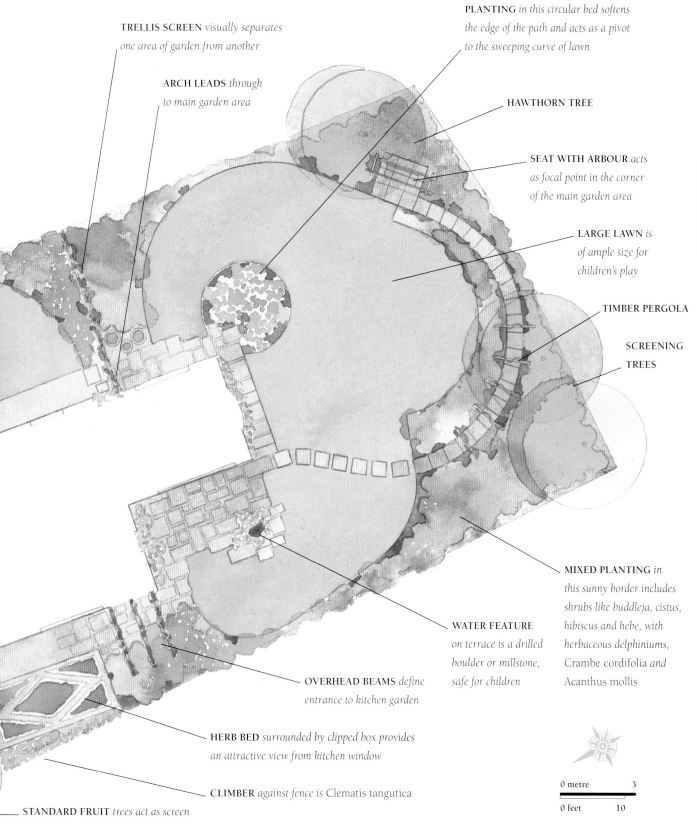

PLANTING *in this circular bed softens the edge of the path and acts as a pivot to the sweeping curve of lawn*

TRELLIS SCREEN *visually separates one area of garden from another*

ARCH LEADS *through to main garden area*

HAWTHORN TREE

SEAT WITH ARBOUR *acts as focal point in the corner of the main garden area*

LARGE LAWN *is of ample size for children's play*

TIMBER PERGOLA

SCREENING TREES

MIXED PLANTING *in this sunny border includes shrubs like buddleja, cistus, hibiscus and hebe, with herbaceous delphiniums, Crambe cordifolia and Acanthus mollis*

WATER FEATURE *on terrace is a drilled boulder or millstone, safe for children*

OVERHEAD BEAMS *define entrance to kitchen garden*

HERB BED *surrounded by clipped box provides an attractive view from kitchen window*

CLIMBER *against fence is Clematis tangutica*

STANDARD FRUIT *trees act as screen*

0 metre   3

0 feet   10

Bold page numbers indicate
illustrations

78

ACKNOWLEDGMENTS

The producers and authors would like to thank the following for their support in the creation of this book: **Mrs P Mitchell**, **Mrs R Hills** and **Victoria Sanders** for allowing us to photograph in their gardens; **Paul Elding** and **Stuart Watson** at Bourne Valley Nurseries, Addlestone, Surrey for their advice, materials and studio; and **John Swithinbank** for all the support and encouragement he gave to Anne.

PICTURE CREDITS
KEY: t = top; b = bottom; l = left; r = right; c = centre; D = designer; G = garden

Neil Campbell-Sharp: G: 32l.
GARDEN FOLIO: **Graham Strong** 38r.
John Glover: G: Toad Hall 14l; G: Chelsea 1992 15b; 20bl; D: Naila Green 42r; G: Holbeach Rd, Shrops 43l; 48l.
HAMILTON PHOTOGRAPHY: **Stephen Hamilton** 31bl, 31br.
HARPUR GARDEN LIBRARY: **Jerry Harpur** G: Barnsley House, Glocs 12r; Diana Ross, London 12l;
Jacqui Hurst: 34br, G: Manor Farm, Lincs 46l;
Andrew Lawson: 22bl, 38l.
CLIVE NICHOLS GARDEN PICTURES: **David Hicks** 24r; G: Mill House,

Sussex 10r; D: Mr & Mrs D Terry 11t; D: Jill Billington 13; D: Gordon White, Austin, Texas 14r; D: Sue Berger 15t; D: Dan Pearson 18t; D: R & J Passmore 19; G: Meadow Plants, Berks 21l; D: Christopher Masson 23; D: Oliva Clarke 25r; Claus Scheinert 25l; G: Coton Manor, Northants 26br; D: Jill Billington 27; D: Randle Siddeley 31t; D: Wendy Lauderdale 32tr; D: R & J Passmore 34bl; 34t; D: Vic Shanley 35l; D: Lucy Gent 35r; D: Jill Billington 37r; D: Jill Billington 39l; G: Butterstream, Eire 40l; D: Nigel Colburn 41l; G: Turn End Garden, Bucks 41r; D: Jill Billington 43r; G: Mill House, Sussex 44; D: Christian Wright 45l; D: E Bristo, Chelsea 1991 45r; D: Julie Toll 46r; 47t; G: Wollerton Hall, Shrops 47b; G: Greystone Hall, Oxon 50l; D: Jill Billington 59r; G: Vale End, Surrey 52; G: Mrs Glaisher, Kent 53.
PHOTOS HORTICULTURAL PICTURE LIBRARY: 21r.
DEREK ST ROMAINE PHOTOGRAPHY: **Derek St Romaine** 9l, 9r, G: Bonita Bulaitis, Hampton Court 1996 22cr; 24b, D: Mark Walker, Chelsea 1996; 26bl, 26tr, 28bl, D: Julie Toll, Chelsea 1996 33bl; G: Wyken Hall 37b; D: Julian Dowel & Jacquie Gordon, Chelsea 1997 39r; 49, **Helen Dillion** 32br.
THE GARDEN PICTURE LIBRARY: **Lynne Brotchie** 36l; **Geoff Dann** 6b; **John Glover** 48r; **Tim Griffith** 18b; **Noel Kavanagh** 51; **Lamontagne** 53r; **Clive Nichols** 6c; **Marie O'Hara** 42l; **Jerry Pavia** 20tl; **Howard Rice** 40r; **JS Sira** 6t, 37tl; **Ron Sutherland** 7, 32; **Brigitte Thomas** 29t, 33r, 36r; **Mel Watson** 32tl.

ADDITIONAL PHOTOGRAPHY: **Steve Gorton** 3, 20tr, 20br, 28tr, 29b, 32tc. **Matthew Ward** 8 all, 11b, 16 all.